S P O R T S

PLUS

POSITIVE LEARNING USING SPORTS

Developing Youth Sports Programs
that Teach Positive Values

Jeffrey Pratt Beedy, Ed.D.

With a Foreword by Dr. Robert Coles

A Project Adventure Publication

Dedication

To God & Family

One of the most significant features we notice in the practice of archery, and in fact all the arts as they are studied in Japan and probably also in other Far Eastern countries, is that they are not intended for utilitarian purposes only or for purely aesthetic enjoyments, but are meant to train the mind, indeed to bring it into contact with the ultimate reality. Archery is, therefore, not practiced solely for the hitting of the target, the swordsman does not wield the sword just for the sake of outdoing his opponent; the dancer does not dance just to perform certain rhythmical movements of the body.

—Eugen Herrigel, *Zen in the Art of Archery*

Foreword

We learn in many ways—a truism, of course, and yet many of us, alas, forget the ironic confines of our educational background: the way we were persuaded that the acquisition of knowledge began and ended in a classroom, or on occasion, the reading room of a library. All the time, however, we are potential teachers of one another, and for children especially, an athletic game can be an occasion for many lessons indeed—emotional and moral, and too, cognitive or factual. Those of us who were active during our high school and college years in a particular sport well remember those moments when something was said or done that lived long and hard in our memories: a gesture, a nod, an effort of one kind or another, a remark—and suddenly a new sense of things, an awareness of this or that, heretofore absent.

In high school I aspired to tennis with almost vehement energy and determination—until, one day, the coach pulled me aside to tell me I was doing "an able, but not a virtuous job!" I wondered what in the world he meant; and he could see my confusion (my ignorance really, with respect to myself, my manner of being). He clarified himself, gave me a casual yet ever so serious lecture on what makes for the proverbial "good sport." To this day I can hear him saying these words: "To win humbly, to lose gracefully, and with a sense of proportion." He lost me at the end, he could see; I had no idea what the word "proportion" had to do with a tennis game gone bad. But he wanted me to stop and think about what truly mattered in life, and why—so I realized as he spoke a few more reflective sentences. He especially wanted that word "humbly" to stick in my mind, to creep into my heart, for I had been on a winning streak; and the pride of it all, the smugness and self-importance had gone to my head. From that day on it was just a little harder for me to strut (though never impossible, I fear)—and even now, I think of that coach ("Fitz" we called him) when something good comes my way. The mastery of foreign languages or mathematics unfortunately was never so instructive.

In this book, Jeffrey Beedy, whom I have known for many years, and who much impressed the college students he taught as a section leader in my course, has given us readers the benefit of his considerable wisdom—his long experience as an athlete, a coach, a teacher, a headmaster, a husband and a father: in all those aspects of living someone trying to heed the famous Emersonian challenge to link the intellect to character, lest we become ever so smart, and not at all good (that is, considerate, kind, generous, sensitive to others in all their possible need or vulnerability). Since any of us is never without a flaw or two, a limitation of thought or feeling, this book will prove invaluable, for sure, to thousands of parents and teachers, and to the young people whom they are meant to instruct and inspire. In page after page we are offered so very much wisdom—hints and suggestions about how we might be more honorable and decent human beings: the biggest challenge of all, and one that the reader will find a more plausible possibility as a consequence of what follows in the chapters ahead.

—*Robert Coles*

Preface

I have been involved with competitive sports for the past 40 years, as an athlete, coach, sports camp owner, researcher, and parent. As you will soon learn, I deeply believe in the value of organized sports for children. In a society that presents our children with so many negative examples, community youth sports programs emerge as a powerful medium for teaching our children important values and skills. As we will explore in this book, however, positive learning does not occur by chance; as adults, we need to assume responsibility for creating positive sports programs.

Sports provided me as a child with an outlet for pent-up afternoon energy. Like many children, I daydreamed about playing professional baseball. Although I never played in the major leagues, I was fortunate to play in the Cape Cod League, which is roughly equivalent to AA ball. In high school I made the Red Sox all–New England Hearst Baseball Team and pitched at Fenway Park. I also played college football and skied in the Freestyle Ski Circuit in the early '70s.

After my competitive career as an athlete, I coached baseball and skiing at a New England prep school. It was during this period of my life that I became interested in the power of sports as a medium for teaching important life skills. As a coach, I was directly involved with my players every afternoon as they struggled with the natural lessons that organized sports offer young people. I shared with my team the frustrations of losing, the joys of winning, and all the emotions that naturally arise as people work and play together toward common goals. After seven years of coaching and teaching, I wanted to learn more about the role of sports in shaping children's lives.

In the early '80s, I began my doctoral studies at Harvard University, where I focused on how children learn and the role that coaches and teachers play in the learning process. After 25 years as an athlete and coach, I was a strong supporter of competitive sports as a positive learning medium for children.

To my surprise, I was soon introduced to the other side of the youth sports story. Many of my doctoral colleagues had had negative sports experiences as children. In fact, some of my respected fellow colleagues and faculty believed that youth sports were terminally negative and suggested that I drop my pursuit of exploring youth sports as a positive learning medium. The idea of competitive sports as a negative influence was new to me; however, I was beginning to realize that my colleagues' experiences were very real and that youth sports were not positive for everyone. In the mid-'80s I found myself at a crossroads. It was at this time that I understood that competitive sports in and of themselves are neither positive nor negative, but a powerful teaching opportunity. It was becoming clear that whether competitive sports are positive or negative depends upon the *quality of the overall program.*

In 1984, I founded an overnight program called the NewSport Experience Camp to explore how sports can be organized to promote positive overall development in children. In 1990 I founded the Positive Learning Using Sports (PLUS) day camp, in Massachusetts, as a way to further explore the role of sports in children's lives. At the Sports PLUS Camp we also introduced the idea of connecting children's love for sports to more traditional academic activities, such as reading and writing. For the next ten years I researched how children learn and develop and how youth sports can be organized to promote positive learning. It was during this period that I began to formalize the basic principles for learning within organized competitive environments. The NewSport Experience Camp and Sports PLUS Camp provided me with a laboratory to test ideas and activities with the goal of developing both good athletes and good people.

A number of interesting themes have emerged as a result of my experience with these camps, my research, and my roles as a parent and as headmaster of a New England coed boarding school. The first is in relation to the NewSport and Sports PLUS Camps and the families that participated. The parents said that they noticed a difference in their children after they returned from the month-long camp. Their children were more cooperative, more focused, and more respectful to their siblings. Many children returned each year and the camp grew in number. As the NewSport Camp grew, we also had the unexpected result of finding that we were incredibly successful in our competition against other camps that were oftentimes two to three times our size. Not only were our campers good people, a major goal of the camp, but we were also more competitive than the other camps.

As I continued my research and practice, I became convinced that being competitive and being a good person are not mutually exclusive goals. As a parent I watched my oldest daughter struggle at the NewSport all-boys camp to develop her passion and confidence as an athlete. Amanda captained three sports in high school and is now playing two sports at a Division III college.

In 1992 I assumed my current position as head of a small coed boarding school in New Hampshire. At New Hampton School our mission is to develop the whole person within the whole community, with a particular focus on being respectful and responsible citizens. With character education as our backdrop, we have also been exceptionally successful in our athletics. In 1996 we won four New England championships in girls' and boys' basketball, skiing, and hockey. At no time was our mission compromised. Our goal to develop good athletes and good people was always our focus.

As a competitive athlete and coach, I believe winning is important. Unlike many who state that youth sports should be only for fun, I think such a philosophy is simplistic and sells our children short. Competitive sports by their very nature pit one team against another with winning as the goal.

If we don't believe that winning is important, we are engaging in wishful and unproductive thinking. A friend of mine, the mother of a 12-year-old Little Leaguer, reminded me that we don't even finish a baseball game when the home team is ahead in the ninth inning. I had never thought of it that way, but to a child the game ends not when the inning is over but when the other team wins the game. This may seem like a simple point, but in a very subtle way it shows by example what is most important.

This is no reason to throw out competition. Instead, we have to realize that, if our children play sports, competition is part of the game. *What we do have control over is what we emphasize, when we emphasize it, and how we shape the learning experience.* At NewSport, we won many more games than we lost, but we never talked about winning. We focused on the process of skill development, continuous improvement, and coordinating our individual efforts toward a common goal. Focusing only on the outcome teaches young children that winning, tournaments, and trophies are the things that matter. The problem with this approach is that the players do not understand the skills, efforts, and planning that lead up to the outcome of winning. Conversely, when we focus on skill mastery, continuous improvement, and teamwork, young children begin to understand that winning takes care of itself. More important, if by unlucky chance an eight-year-old plays poorly on a team that keeps winning, she will be less likely to experience false confidence. Equally important, if the same player improves her bunting and fielding skills each game and contributes to a team that keeps losing, she has good reasons to feel confident.

The genesis of this book was my interest in playing sports as a child. Although as a young player I was unaware of the educational benefits of playing sports, the lessons I learned guide my life as a parent, coach, and educator. At eight years old I didn't think about abstract concepts such as respect, responsibility, and teamwork. Like most eight-year-old Little Leaguers, I just wanted to play. As I reflect on my early experiences in competitive sports, however, I now realize that these early introductions to team play provided me with skills and values that have carried over to other areas of life. Later, when I became a coach, I realized the incredible power the leader of a team can possess for developing athletes and people. As coaches we are in a position to shape how our players come to understand the same important values we learned as children. For better or worse, the coach holds the power to teach skills that will ultimately have more value than executing a perfect suicide squeeze.

As an educator interested in the development of positive character values in our children, I believe that organized youth sports provide a unique opportunity to make a difference in young people's lives. In addition to all the reasons I have just mentioned, youth sports programs are refreshingly free of many of the political pressures that constrict teachers and school systems. Many educators would agree that, since the publication of *A Nation at Risk* in 1983, little progress has been made in educational reform. Organized activities such as sports provide a relatively uncharted domain for implementing most of the educational models heralded as critical to preparing our children for the 21st century. Most youth sports programs, for instance, are not shackled by unions and boards that scrutinize every new curriculum or program. In this sense, sports offer an important entry point for proactive community leaders to affect the lives of children.

The underlying reason for writing this book is to make a positive difference in children's lives. There are many worthwhile avenues to accomplish such a goal. With the number of young children playing organized sports and the unique educational opportunities that sports provide, I am confident that the effort of writing this book has been worthwhile. My deepest wish is that this book will guide the adults who have accepted the incredibly important role of teaching and coaching our young people.

—Jeffrey Pratt Beedy Ed.D.

Acknowledgments

———————————————— ■ ————————————————

First of all, thank-you, God, for my mom, dad, sister and my modest talents as an athlete. My family were very important forces in my early years, nurturing my love for sports and the outdoors. There were many others who shaped my early years as an athlete and coach, including Jack Jones, John Coughlin, Roger Page, Dana Wallace, Bruce Kingdon, Tom Stevenson, Tom Cortapassi, Tom Reynolds, Don Jacobs and Hobie Ellis.

It is also important to thank all those people who believed in me and the PLUS concept early on. I owe a great deal of thanks to my mentors, Jerry Pieh and Peter Zoch, in shaping my life as an educator and developer of the Sports PLUS Model. I owe a deep debt of gratitude to Lawrence Kohlberg, Bob Selman, Terry Tividen and Gil Noam for supporting my research at Harvard. Thank you Carol Gilligan, Lyn Minkel-Brown, Mark Tappin, Dawn Schrader for your insight and support in my first attempts to create a sports-education model. Special thanks to Ed Foley, David Rost, Jane Haynes, Holly Metcalf, Keith Lee, Luis Tiant, Marjorie Nance, Irene Waas, Diane Proctor, Jane Brewer, Frank Millet and Tom Flaherty for your role in launching the Sports PLUS camp at Milton Academy.

Special thanks to Robert Coles and Tom Lickona for providing me with vision and mentorship.

I also want to thank my many friends who have supported my efforts over the years including Jon Marcus, Mark Tilton, Steve Lapin, Ed Netter, Warren Cook, David Britton, Gerret Warner, J.D. Sloan, Steve Hardy, Steve Ables, Lee Simes, John Ritzo, Ester Hearn, David Fowler, Peter Yarrow, Jonann Torsey, Tom Abbott, John Gordon, David Smith, John Hazelton, Gary and Kathy Beban, Joan Benoit-Samuelson and Peter Beach.

A very special thanks to my PLUS partners Joe Bowab, Cindy Glidden, Dean Gardner, Gara Field, DJ Glusker and Luke Beatty.

An important thank-you is in order to Bob Kennedy, Jason Pilalas, A. B. Whitfield and my entire New Hampton School Board of Trustees for their incredible support .

We are all fortunate for the existence of organizations like Project Adventure. Thank you, Project Adventure, for supporting the PLUS Model and publishing my book. I believe deeply in the philosophy of Adventure Education. More importantly, I respect and trust the wonderful people involved, past and present, including Dick Prouty, Jerry Pieh, Lisa Furlong, Tom Zierk and the rest of the P.A. team.

I feel blessed that I had the opportunity to work with Tom Zierk. He is one of the kindest human beings I have had the pleasure of knowing. Thank you Tom for your guidance, humor, insight, friendship and most of all, patience. We were a great team.

Keith Sidel provided the illustrations for this book. His ability to bring the various personalities to life is amazing. Thanks, Keith.

The biggest thanks goes to my wife, Anne, and daughters Amanda and Bailey for supporting me over the past decade as I finally put my ideas into written word. I love you.

Thanks to my friend and running partner, Casey.

A final thanks to all mentioned and those I failed to mention for your inspiration. The threads of your work and love weave their way throughout the fabric of this book.

Introduction

In thinking of how to present the information contained in this book, we went through several attempts before settling on this final version. The most difficult task was deciding on the order in which to present the stages and components of the PLUS (Positive Learning Using Sports) model. At first, the sections on philosophy and values and how children learn were presented before the PLUS cycle of Warm-Up/Activity/Cool-Down. But after getting the same feedback from several coaches who previewed the book, we reversed the order, presenting the PLUS cycle first.

We originally thought that coaches first needed to consider and develop their coaching philosophy and team values. What we found, however, was that coaches found the PLUS cycle to be something they could immediately put to use in their programs. After using the principles of the cycle to provide a structure—a sports classroom—in which learning naturally occurs, these coaches could begin discussing team philosophy and values with the children on their teams.

Heeding the advice to *let the game instruct,* we settled on a practical approach to structuring the book. We followed the PLUS model, specifically the learning cycle of Warm-Up/Activity/Cool-Down.

The Warm-Up

The first two chapters provide background information and an introduction to the PLUS model. Chapter One describes the important role youth sports can play in the development of children. There is also a discussion of some of the most loaded issues in youth sports—winning, losing, and competition. Chapter Two introduces the PLUS model and its various components. These chapters set the stage for the Activity portion of the book, which is divided into four sections, like a youth soccer game.

First Quarter—The PLUS Learning Cycle

The three chapters in this section follow the three phases of the learning cycle. This is the core structure of the PLUS model and presents a format that coaches can immediately incorporate into their programs. By following the structure of the cycle, coaches can provide an environment in which their young athletes feel safe both physically and emotionally. The discussion portions of the cycle give children a chance to explore issues with their teammates and coaches.

The Warm-Up, Chapter Three, presents the first portion of the cycle. This short, five- to ten-minute team meeting precedes every practice and game. It is a time for children to transition to the coming activity and discuss goals, game strategies, skill drills, or any issue they need to talk about. Chapter Four goes on to the Activity portion of the cycle. It is during this phase—the game or practice—that coaches look for teachable moments, naturally occurring incidents that give concrete examples of lessons we want children to learn. Children can far better understand an incidence of disrespect in someone's behavior than in a lecture. Chapter Five shows how a post-game or -practice Cool-Down meeting allows children opportunities to discuss their thoughts and emotions immediately following an activity. This provides children and coaches with a time to discuss and learn lessons from the game or practice while it is still fresh in their minds.

Second Quarter—Three Ways Children Learn

Understanding some of the ways in which children learn helps coaches become more effective teachers who positively influence children's lives. Chapter Six discusses the powerful role coaches play in the quality of the experiences children have participating in youth sports. Chapter Seven explores the importance of interactive dialogue to children's development. The structure of the PLUS cycle provides time for children to develop dialogue skills and to discuss ideas and issues. This promotes intellectual development and decision-making abilities. Rewards and consequences, and how coaches can use them to encourage positive values, are discussed in Chapter Eight.

Third Quarter—Philosophy and Values

Have you ever asked yourself why you coach or what you want your children to learn playing youth sports? Developing a personal philosophy of youth sports is an important first step for any coach to take. Knowing how you prioritize such potentially conflicting issues as winning versus equal playing time will go a long way toward making sure you provide a good experience for your players. Chapter Nine presents and discusses the ten items of the PLUS philosophy. It also asks coaches to think about and then develop a team philosophy with their players. Chapter Ten takes this exercise to the next level by bringing your philosophy to life. Using the five core values of the PLUS model, coaches can begin teaching children what it looks like to be responsible, to be respectful, and to be a contributing member of a team.

Fourth Quarter—Developmental Stages

Many children begin participating in organized youth sports programs as young as five years old. The ways in which they relate to each other, the coach, and the game itself change greatly as they get older. For coaches to be effective, they must understand not only the physical abilities of their athletes but also their intellectual and psychological constraints and capabilities. Chapter 11 discusses what to expect when coaching children under the age of eight, and the special attention coaches need to pay when introducing complex and difficult concepts to them, like what it means to really play together as a team. Chapter 12 continues to track children's development from ages eight to ten. While they make great strides both physically and mentally, children at this age still may not fully understand the complexities of team sports. Chapter 13 looks at children ages ten to twelve, and how their understanding of sports becomes more team- and skill-oriented. All of these chapters provide coaches with guidelines for working with their particular age group and how to be certain that their expectations match the children's capabilities.

The Cool-Down

The final chapters of the book move beyond the everyday experience to challenge our thinking about youth sports. Chapter 14 reexamines some of our commonly held beliefs about sports: Do sports really build character? Is competition good or bad? What is wrong with wanting to win? Chapter 15 asks which lessons learned from sports can be transferred beyond the playing fields. What can children do to give back to the community that provides their sports experience for them? The chapter concludes with a look at a model program that incorporates the natural interest many children have in sports to enhance their literacy.

Contents

The Warm-Up

Positive Learning Using Sports

Today many of us experience sports through the eyes and hearts of our children. We rush off to soccer practices and basketball games. We find ourselves standing next to our neighbors cheering our children on as they begin their young careers as competitve athletes. But what are our children learning beyond how to kick, or hit, or throw a ball? What do we want them to learn? How much control do we have, as parents and coaches, over these early sports experiences?

In this first section, The Warm-Up, we will consider these and other important questions, how and what many children are currently learning in their first sports experience, and how we can create programs that actively promote positive learning.

CHAPTER ONE

Tapping The Potential of Youth Sports

At the end of a recent soccer match, two players from Coach Goodsport's second-grade team showed more interest in being first in the congratulating line than in participating in the cheer for their opponents. As the two boys raced away from the huddle, Coach Goodsport called the boys over and quietly asked them to go to the end of the line. Surprised, the boys moved to the back.

At the team's post-game Cool-Down meeting, Coach Goodsport congratulated her team on a game well played. "I'm proud of the way you worked hard together and kept pushing the ball up the field, even after we missed a couple of shots. You showed a lot of teamwork and perseverance. And you all did better on defense and clearing the ball from our end of the field. Remember, that was our team goal for this game."

She allowed some enthusiastic response from the players before bringing up a new topic. "Can anyone tell me what the word *appreciate* means?" A few children attempted to explain. "Well, it means that, you know, that you appreciate somebody." "You like what they did." "It's like you are thanking them."

Coach Goodsport realized that while they couldn't articulate it, they knew what it means to appreciate somebody. She then asked why they give the cheer—*Two, four, six, eight! Who do we appreciate!*

While the children struggled to answer, Coach Goodsport helped out. "Would a game be much fun to play if the other team didn't show up?" "NO!" shouted the team. "Would it be fun if the other team didn't try very hard?" "NO!" "How about if the other team played really rough or cheated?" "NO!"

She saw that the children understood her point and let them comment. "We are telling the other team that we appreciate them for playing a good game and for being good sports." "And we appreciate them because without them we wouldn't have had any fun cause we wouldn't have even played the game!"

Coach Goodsport went on for another moment, reminding her players that the purpose of giving the cheer was to let the opposing players know that their effort was appreciated. She then pointed out that by not participating in the cheer, players were not respecting their opponents, or their teammates, and reminded them that respect was one of the values their team had agreed was important. She went on to say that they all should participate in the cheer and not worry about being first in the congratulating line.

The whole Cool-Down session took seven minutes.

❖

There are a number of ways that Coach Goodsport could have handled this situation. She could have scolded the two boys in front of the other players. She could have taken them off to the side to talk to them. She could have ignored the situation altogether. But Coach Goodsport recognizes the tremendous potential that sports have to teach children lessons about such things as respect, responsibility, perseverance, fair play, and teamwork. She looks for *teachable moments,* observable actions that present tangible expressions of these otherwise abstract concepts.

Coach Goodsport has used the PLUS (Positive Learning Using Sports) model to create an environment in which her players feel safe both emotionally and physically, safe to share their thoughts and feelings without fear of being laughed at or put down. She has created a structure that gives her players time to discuss their performance in games and practices, issues of interest and concern to the children, and incidents like the above. Within this structure—this sports classroom—the children know that they will be treated fairly, kindly, and with respect, regardless of their individual athletic ability.

"We obtain better knowledge of a person during one hour's play and games than by conversing with him for a whole year."

— *Plato*

Tapping the Potential

We all hope that our children will benefit from playing on a sports team. What parent would not want their child to learn positive character values from playing on a youth sports team? Even more, what if their children learned how to attach those values to specific behaviors and attitudes and then began to transfer those behaviors to life away from the playing field?

Sports in and of themselves are neither positive nor negative. Simply playing youth soccer does not guarantee that a child will learn to be respectful of others or to be a responsible team member. In fact, we are becoming increasingly aware that all too often a child's early sports experience teaches the wrong things—how to cheat, inflated egos for some, with low self-esteem for others, how to hurt opponents both physically and emotionally, and a winning-is-the-only-thing mentality.

Whether sports contribute to positive or negative learning depends on the role we—parents and coaches—take in shaping our children's sports programs. That sports teach values is beyond debate. Children do learn values

from playing organized sports. The question is whether we will choose to take responsibility for influencing which values are learned and the way in which this learning occurs.

Creating The Sports Classroom

Although youth sports provide tremendous potential for growth, certain educational practices are necessary for positive learning to occur. The purpose of this book is to show, through a step-by-step process, how coaches and parents can create and maintain a positive environment where children can learn the lessons that we believe are important—a sports classroom in which children feel safe to grow and challenge themselves socially, physically, and intellectually, regardless of their athletic abilities.

Like an academic classroom, a sports classroom must have a structure that promotes rules of behavior and values that the children, parents, and coaches agree on, and a teacher who models these behaviors and values. A coach has more of an impact on the overall psychological development of the child than playing the sport does. This is a key point. As a coach, you must think of yourself as a teacher, with the opportunity to shape the children's learning.

Teachers understand that many children learn best through "experience and doing," especially when we provide them with time to reflect on and discuss their experiences. Creative teachers recognize that this method of teaching is more effective than lecturing. The same is true of learning through sports. In the opening story Coach Goodsport recognized an educational opportunity, what we refer to as a *teachable moment*. A teachable moment is an every day occurrence that can be captured and used to teach something, in this case the value of respect. Instead of lecturing, Coach Goodsport employed a Cool-Down session, part of the structure that she uses to provide time for her players to discuss and reflect on important issues and concerns.

Teaching and learning are not passive. Coach Goodsport took a proactive educational approach to learning. Had she not addressed the situation of the boys running to the head of the line, what would the children have learned from it, if anything? It's actually pretty simple: If we want to make sure that sports are in the positive educational realm, we have to be proactive in our approach. This is what the Sports PLUS model is all about—it offers coaches and parents a structure that ensures their children's first sports experience will be a positive one.

What Sports Can Teach

Organized youth sports are often overlooked as a medium for teaching and learning. Sports are viewed primarily as physical activities, games of stamina and skill. But to fully tap the rich learning medium sports represent, we must recognize that sports are also social, cognitive, and moral activities.

> **Social Activity**—First and foremost, sports are essentially a social undertaking. They involve teams—groups of individuals coming together to play in shared activity. Because preadolescents begin to spend a tremendous amount of time in the company of their peers, team sports are both important and relevant to children's development. Within the mini-society of a team, children interact, play, fight, and make friends, actions that provide an important context for their development. The varied levels of interaction in

sports provide a rich setting for children to observe and learn about human relations and responsibility.

Cognitive Activity—Sport are also as much cognitive activities as they are social. As contest-based games, sports involve thinking through a strategy—reacting and acting to your teammates and opponents. Participants must interpret a situation and imagine a possible course of action. They must begin to learn to think through their actions and to "see" the field and game, even when they are not directly involved in the action. Watch any group of young children play soccer and you will notice that the players all swarm towards the ball. Young children often interpret events from their own point of view. Older children, on the other hand, usually show more passing and cooperative play as their perspectives widen.

Moral Activity—During a soccer game, you, the coach, are standing at the sideline with your players who are waiting to go into the game. The ball is kicked out of bounds, right next to you. You clearly saw who last touched the ball and so did your players— it was last touched by a player on your team. But the ref, a 14-year-old high school student, did not have a clear view of the play and awards the ball to your team—the wrong call. The players are all looking at you expectantly, wondering, waiting. What will you do?

How a player or coach resolves a conflict and why a particular course of action is right are important questions sports present us with. In this example, your decision, regardless of which course of action you take, must be explainable to the children. Whether it's "The ref is always right" or you quietly point out to the ref how you saw the play, your decision must be understood by the children. The sports experience is filled with ethical issues—issues that confront participants with choices of how they should act. With their rules, relationships, and fluid action, sports are an excellent vehicle for exercising ethical and moral thought.

Winning and Competition

Before we look in more detail at the PLUS model, let's address the issues of winning and competition. I want to do this right up front, because rarely will you get into a more lively discussion with parents of children playing sports

■ *Keep It Fun*

Creating a climate of fun for your team means that the children will practice and play harder and take a personal interest in their team, in each other, and in their own learning. It will make a big difference in how the children play—as a team or simply as a group of individuals—if all your players truly enjoy the sports experience you create for them.

than over these issues. Winning and competition will be discussed throughout this book and in greater detail in Chapter Fourteen, but since this is such a controversial topic, I'd like to take a few minutes to give you my take on it.

Numerous sports studies show that the number one reason children play sports is to have fun. Period. In most studies, winning shows up around number eight or ten. The unfortunate truth is that we adults have created the overly competitive, winning-is-everything environment. I remember how differently the young players acted at my sports camp in Maine when their parents weren't around. When the kids were on their own, without the influence of the parents on the sidelines, they supported their teammates. In most cases, they wanted their friends to play more than they wanted to win. When parents' weekend came around, the attitudes of the kids visibly changed—they were reacting to their parents' presence.

Where Do You Stand?

On one side of the debate are those who think this whole idea of positive learning is soft; we need to toughen up our kids for the *real world*. If they don't make the Little League cut or the travel team, then that is a positive lesson. If it doesn't kill them, then it makes them better! On the other side are those who wonder whether our youth sports programs have become too focused on winning, uniforms, and tournaments. Youth sports should just be fun, they remind us.

Whichever side of the debate you tend to lean toward, we must wrestle with these divergent views. You cannot simply pretend that winning and losing can be removed from the process. Here's a statement that should add fuel to the fire: I believe that every time your children step onto the field your intention should be to win. If you do not feel that way, you are short changing you players. Here's my point: winning is not necessarily evil. What can happen is that we become so obsessed with winning as the only result of a game that we lose sight of the process—the striving for excellence, the pushing of oneself to reach new goals, improve on and learn new skills, and break through perceived limitations. If we look at competition as a process, a chance to become better at something, then the end result, win or lose, becomes less important. Whatever is achieved or learned in preparing for the contest is not lost, and serves to make us better than we were.

Winning and losing are the end results of any athletic competition. They are a measure of a particular activity, but they are not the only measure. The importance of winning needs to be understood within the context of what factors contribute to it. If a team of kids practices hard, plays well as a team, executes the skills they practice, and consistently sets higher levels and works toward them, they will likely achieve some measure of success—they will win games. But what happens when they meet up with a nine-year-old future major league pitcher who throws 50-mile-an-hour fastballs? The point is, the children on your team have control only over how *they* play. In this case, winning will be unlikely. How they meet this challenge, what they learn, and how they improve through the process become the greatest measures of their success.

A Matter of Emphasis

Our society has a fixation with *winning* that goes way beyond sports. Without getting into a long-winded philosophical discussion on this misplaced prominence, we at least need to consider how winning and losing fit into the context of youth sports.

As stated in the Sports PLUS philosophy (Chapters Two and Nine), winning, at number ten on the list, should be seen merely as the end result of the game. Try this. Take the word win out of your vocabulary. Now describe a game, let's use baseball, with a score of Cougars 12, Badgers 10. Remember, you cannot use the word win. You could say the Cougars beat the Badgers, but let's take beat and anything synonymous out of our vocabulary too. Now you can say that the score at the end of the game was 12 to 10. What this simple twist of language does is to make you look at the score as just a piece within the greater context of the game.

While this may seem like a simplistic way of dealing with the whole loaded notion of winning and losing, placing emphasis on the final score rather than on who won and who lost allows you to use the score to analyze how your team did in terms of goals and skill improvement. The score, whether your team won or lost, becomes a benchmark from which you can begin discussing

■ *Is Fair Always Equal?*

The question whether fairness always means equality can be understood from a developmental perspective. For example, I don't think that we should worry about putting the best players in late in the game when we are talking about children under ten. Why? Because research and experience show that kids develop at different rates, and the apparently less talented nine-year-old hitter can easily develop into the best 12-year-old hitter in a few short years. To reward perceived talent disproportionately at this early age risks encouraging a lack of confidence in some children.

On the other hand, if an unathletic, relatively weak 10-year-old is due up to bat against a pitcher who is throwing uncontrolled 50-mile-an-hour fastballs, you need to understand the danger—both physical and psychological. The coach needs to consider the situation, the players, and the team philosophy and make a call based on common sense.

with your team their performance during the game. Maybe they scored 12 runs and the other team only scored 10, but the goals of making better cutoffs and backing up positions on infield hits were not achieved. Had they been, the other team would only have scored eight runs.

And if your team was on the 10-run end of the final score, this again offers you a place to begin to analyze your team's performance. Their cutoffs and backing up of positions were done inconsistently and allowed four runs. Had they done better with their goals, they might have kept the other team to eight runs.

The goal is to de-emphasize winning and losing and emphasize skill development and continuous improvement. Focusing on the score allows the kids to have a conclusion to their game while helping them to see whichever side of the score they are on as place from which to analyze their performance.

It helps kids at this age to have the pressure to win taken off. A fun way to deal with the pressure that can quickly become part of the team culture is the inside joke that this team does not use the words win, lose, beat, etc. Come up with some silly consequences for a player on your team who uses any of the taboo words. And be sure to have the kids help decide what these consequences should be. I guarantee they will come up with some interesting ones.

Summary

My intention is that this book will provide a model for coaches and parents that will ensure that the lessons our children learn from their first sports experiences will be positive. Sports can be either beneficial or harmful. The main focus of this book is that the lessons learned, both positive and negative, depend on the values modeled by parents and coaches and the foundation upon which the children's sports experience is built. *Children will learn something* from the games they play. The intention of this book is to help interested adults—both parents and community coaches—create an environment in which children feel safe to learn and grow in positive ways.

CHAPTER TWO

The PLUS Approach

On this Saturday, Coach Win-At-All-Costs' soccer team is playing Coach Goodsport's team. Coach Win-At-All-Costs tells parents that sports build character. Early season talk sounds great, and the kids are hoping to win the championship. Coach Win-At-All-Costs tells his players that they are all a part of the same team, so they need to work together.

Before the game starts, Coach Goodsport brings her team together for a Warm-Up meeting to discuss goals for the game and to listen to her athletes' concerns. She outlines today's goals: focusing on fellow team-mates' ideas and performances and clearing the ball from their end of the field. She explains how the goals can be accomplished: "All comments will be directed to our players; remember to use first names; let's hear comments like 'Good work, Amy. Nice shot, Sam. Excellent pass, Tommy. And remember the clearing and passing drills we've been working on in practice."

During the game, Tommy Too-Cool begins to hog the ball and trash talk the opposing team. Coach Goodsport takes Tommy aside and asks him to repeat what the goals were in the Warm-Up meeting. Tommy says he was not paying attention. Coach Goodsport acknowledges this and says that he can make amends by sitting on the bench and helping his teammates with the team goals. Tommy participates in making positive comments to his teammates and his behavior is rewarded with another chance to play in the second half. After the game, Coach Goodsport pulls the team together for a Cool-Down meeting and reviews the game. During this meeting Tommy talks about what he has learned.

On the other side of the field, Coach Win-At-All-Costs tells his team how pleased he is that they have won by a team effort. Many of the children are happy because they beat an undefeated team. However, not everyone is happy. Because the game was close, and Coach Win-At-All-Costs wanted to win, Timid Teresa played only four minutes, all in the last quarter. Her enthusiasm is beginning to wane, and she tells her mother she does not want to go to next Saturday's game. Teresa's mother is worried that she might not want to play soccer anymore. Teresa is wondering if she is really a part of the team.

"Children may soon forget what you say, but they will never forget how you make them feel."

Teresa and Tommy are both learning something about themselves and others. Tommy is beginning to understand the value of teamwork and the importance of being respectful to others. Unfortunately, Teresa is learning that some adults value winning more than keeping their word. Both teams here are learning values—the question is what values are they learning? As coaches we, need to capture the potential of youth sports. The PLUS model provides a structure for creating an environment where children can learn positive character values.

Creating The PLUS Environment

In the stories that open these first two chapters, we see the climate Coach Goodsport has created for her team. The children feel safe physically, psychologically, and socially. Her players know that they will all be treated fairly and given equal opportunity to play. The youngsters may not be able to fully articulate what they like about playing on Coach Goodsport's team, but they know how good it makes them feel.

Children need a climate in which they feel comfortable and safe, where they feel confident to push themselves in new directions without fear of ridicule or being put down. The result is that the children have fun and learn more. Not surprisingly, this type of environment increases the potential for winning (The Secret Weapon).

■ *The Secret Weapon*

An added bonus, consistently proven true over my years of coaching and research, is that if you follow the PLUS principles you will win more games. As the field of sports psychology has discovered, the likelihood of winning is enhanced when harmony, teamwork, and continuous improvement are the goals. Teams whose players respect one another and understand the true notion of teamwork will consistently beat more talented but individually oriented teams. This is what I refer to as the secret weapon of youth sports.

The PLUS Model

The PLUS model can be understood as three pieces working together to build a positive learning environment. Each piece consists of principles and practical tools.

1. The PLUS Learning Cycle
2. Three Ways that Children Learn
3. Philosophy and Values

The PLUS Learning Cycle

We have all attended youth sports practices and games where things seem a bit chaotic. The players are all over the field. The equipment is strewn all over the sideline. Two players are squabbling about who bats next. One is climbing the fence. The coach is yelling, but no one seems to be listening. What teacher would ever dream of running a classroom like this?

The PLUS approach suggests that, much like an academic classroom, the sports environment can be organized in ways that enhance learning. Instead of chaos, the PLUS Learning Cycle provides coaches with a structure that incorporates effective principles of learning. It offers practical tools for creating an environment in which children quickly feel comfortable and coaches can effectively teach.

The PLUS Learning Cycle consists of three phases: the Warm-Up, the Activity, and the Cool-Down, or pre–during–after game segments. This structure provides coaches with an organized classroom-like setting.

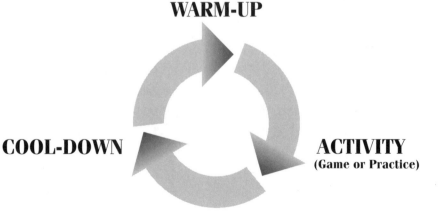

■ *Warm-Up*

The five-to ten-minute pre-game or pre-practice team meeting is the time when the coach outlines goals and game strategies, and engages the players in interactive dialogue. It offers a quiet time for the children's transition from what they have been doing to focusing on the coming Activity.

■ *Activity*

The Activity is another name for a game or practice. It is during the Activity portion of the PLUS Cycle that coaches look for teachable moments that offer concrete examples of abstract concepts.

■ *Cool-Down*

The Cool-Down provides the coach and the players with an opportunity to revisit the goals set during the Warm-Up, discuss how the team performed during the game or practice, and set new goals. It is also a time to address teachable moments observed during the Activity. The Cool-Down is reflective in nature and provides the best opportunity for active dialogue.

Three Ways That Children Learn

The second piece of the PLUS model looks at ways in which children learn. Understanding how children learn in the sports environment will help you shape the learning process to be a more effective teacher.

Educational psychology suggests there are at least three distinct ways people learn within an environment such as organized sports. We refer to these three areas as the *Principles of Learning.*

■ *Modeling*

Research shows that a coach can have a greater impact on the psychological development of children than the sport itself. For this reason, the PLUS model stresses the notion that children learn by watching. How do you respond to losing? What do you say when the referee makes a bad call? Do you say one thing and do another? How do you administer discipline? Do you preach sportsmanship yet swear under your breath? The PLUS model states that how we act is more important than what we say. Your players are watching your every move. If you want to encourage respect you must model respect. It is as simple as that.

■ *Dialogue*

Another way children learn is through discussing important issues with people they look up to and feel comfortable with. How much time do you spend in conversation with your players? Do you do all the talking? Do you encourage them to think? Have you created an environment where children are encouraged to respectfully argue their ideas? Do you empower your players or do you need to be in control? Values such as respect and responsibility are best learned when children are empowered and have opportunities to engage in mutual dialogue.

The main purpose of the PLUS Warm-Up and Cool-Down sessions is to encourage mutual dialogue among players and coaches. This interactive discussion is fundamentally different from the standard "coach's pep talk" in that mutual dialogue exercises the mind, encouraging intellectual, social, and moral development.

■ *Rewards*

A third important way of learning is through rewards and consequences. What do you reward? Do you subtly treat the better players differently? What are your policies and rules? What values do your rules support? Do you enforce your rules evenly? When a coach says that swearing is wrong, yet allows the best athlete to swear, the other players will be watching and learning.

Philosophy and Values

The philosophy of a team forms the foundation of what that team believes to be most important. Decisions about playing time, selection of teams, personal relations, and the issues of winning and losing rest on your philosophy regarding children and youth sports. Your team's values grow out of its philosophy, translating it into actions that are observable and measurable in the behavior of coaches, players, and even parents.

Philosophy

The PLUS philosophy provides the principles that guide day-to-day activities and decisions. The PLUS model consists of the following philosophical principles.

1. Sports should promote self-confidence.

2. Sports should encourage the development of character values such as teamwork, respect, responsibility, fair play, and perseverance.

3. Playing time should be distributed evenly.

4. Positions should be distributed evenly.

5. Rules and consequences should be clearly spelled out and enforced fairly and consistently.

6. Coaches and parents must model the values they want their children to learn.

7. It is our responsibility to help all children realize their personal potential.

8. Respect and responsibility are the basis of the moral fabric of a team.

9. Teaching the whole child requires the involvement of the whole community.

10. Winning and losing are only the end result of a game.

Values

Values bring your philosophy to life. The PLUS model is organized around five universal core values. These five values represent a common set of principles we can all agree are important—values that transcend culture, religion, or socio economic differences. Moreover, they are themes that are powerfully communicated through the action of team sports.

While there are other important values to teach children, I have identified these five as basic building blocks. Associated with them are other important values or sub-themes. For example, along with respect we find kindness, compassion, and tolerance; responsibility includes trustworthiness, hard work, and

VALUE	
What it is	**What it looks like**

Respect

Regard for the dignity and worth of all persons (including self). Treat all people as individuals; accept human differences.	Care and respect oneself (body and mind) and others—both teammates and opponents. Do not participate in "trash talking" or other conduct that is likely to hurt others.

Responsibility

Being accountable for one's actions—to self and others; acknowledging duties to self and others.	Strive for your personal best, both on and off the playing field. Be reliable and dependable to your teammates, coaches, and parents.

Teamwork

Work and cooperate with others toward mutual goals; stress collaboration over self-interest. Embrace the values of respect and responsibility.	Combining the diverse talents and skills of each team member to achieve a common goal. One important measure of success is in how well a team plays together.

Fair Play

Refers to equity and the rights of individuals; underscores the importance of following rules and principles.	Follow the rules of the game, both written and unwritten. Play fair; never cheat or play unfairly to gain an advantage over an opponent. Recognize that your opponent wants the same things you do.

Perseverance

Keep trying in spite of setbacks, disappointments, or opposition; stay determined and focused on pursuing one's goals and dreams.	Don't worry about a bad shot or poor performance. Learn from mistakes, move on, and look forward to the next opportunity.

loyalty; fair play involves honesty, equality, and justice; teamwork includes respect, responsibility, and cooperation; and perseverance includes courage, self-discipline, and dedication.

Any one of these principles in isolation will not necessarily encourage growth. The value of the PLUS model is that it provides a structure for coaches to use in addressing the principles in an integrated way, through specific, observable instances—teachable moments. For many if not most children, these principles are abstract and difficult to grasp. Sports provides action and context to the principles. Using the PLUS model helps children learn to recognize these concepts in action and then begin to model them.

How Will I Find The Time?

Isn't it the coach's goal to teach sports skills? Won't spending time talking with the children about issues like respect and teamwork take time away from teaching skills and strategies? These are natural questions; however, the PLUS model creates an environment conducive to getting more done. Creating a positive environment will save you time organizing practices and allow you more time to spend teaching skills.

You may initially feel that you are spending too much time having group discussions with your kids. But stick with it. Once your young athletes get used to the PLUS environment, they will focus sooner, pay attention longer, and work harder—all with less direction and shouting by you.

Summary

The PLUS approach combines relevant research in educational theory with practical experience in youth sports to create a positive environment that encourages growth in children. Using the structure of the PLUS cycle creates a climate for your team in which children will feel safe both physically and emotionally. Within this environment, this sports classroom, you will have opportunities to use the ways in which children learn and develop positive character values. Like the ingredients of a cake, all the parts of the PLUS model are important to the quality of the final product. Ultimately, the Sports PLUS approach is about creating a sports experience where children can grow and develop both as athletes and as people. With positive growth as our goal, we are on the right track for tapping the potential of youth sports.

The PLUS Cycle

Not many people will disagree with the idea of using sports as a medium to teach children positive character values. The big question becomes how? Coaches are charged by the parents of the children on their teams with providing a sports experience—how to kick, how to throw, how to hit, how to play with teammates. And all this usually in a limited amount of time with a group of athletes enabled with short attention spans and easily distracted.

The PLUS Cycle presents a structure that coaches can immediately implement into their programs. It provides a framework for building a positive learning environment, where children will actually focus sooner, pay attention longer, and have opportunities to discuss valuable lessons.

CHAPTER THREE

The Warm-Up

One by one the Cougars arrive at the local park. The sun is still strong on this early July night and the players have been thinking about their game all day. Tonight Coach Parent's Cougars play Coach Neophyte's Rockets. Quietly Coach Parent gathers his team into a semicircle and raises his hand. Gordon is the first to raise his hand and Josh follows. The team becomes quiet, and the children begin to focus their attention on Coach Parent.

"Charlie, can you please round up Jared and Ken for our Warm-Up session. Hi, team, it's good to see you tonight. Johnny can I please have your attention. Ken, please put the bat on the rack and join us. Thanks, Ken.

How is everybody doing?"

"Awesome!"

"Remember last practice? During our Cool-Down session we all agreed we wanted to work on two things during this game. Does anyone remember what our two goals were?"

"Yeah, we wanted to win our next game," yells Tommy.

"Well," replies Coach Parent, "we did all agree we wanted to win, but we also agreed that if we focused on two important things the winning would take care of itself—does anybody remember what those two things are?"

Josh raises his hand. "We need to work on our cutoffs from the outfield."

"Good," says Coach Parent. "We allowed four unearned runs because we threw the ball away."

"We also said we were going to work on being responsible team members," Tommy suddenly remembers.

"Could you give me an example of how we can be responsible?"

"Keeping the bats lined up when we are on the bench, coaching first base when we are at bat without being asked, and bringing the team together after the game for a Cool-Down without you having to remind us."

"Good," said Coach Parent. "Lining up the bats, coaching first base, and bringing the team together after the game—especially on your own without me asking—are good examples of being responsible team members. For today's game I want you to work on making accurate throws to the cutoff person and to do one responsible act during the game. We will use the Cool-Down session to talk about our goals. During the Cool-Down I will ask everyone to share what they did to be responsible. Be sure you're ready. I also want you to think of other ways you can be responsible as team members. Think about what else needs to be done during the game. What about before the game? How can you be a leader as responsible team member?"

———————————— ❖ ————————————

So went the Warm-Up session.

Coach Parent understands that children learn best in an environment that is organized and safe, and where players and coaches are respectful to one another. Using some simple techniques, he was able to create a climate—

a sports classroom—where positive learning happens naturally. Viewed in this light, the sports experience is not unlike the atmosphere of an academic classroom in which children are excited about learning and feel safe to grow and explore their own physical, intellectual, and social development.

Coach Parent did a good job of organizing an often chaotic moment into one that is conducive to teaching and learning. What were some of the important ingredients that provided the foundation for Coach Parent's Warm-Up session? How did he round up the team? How did he focus the ten-year-olds on their goals? In a relatively short time Coach Parent got the players to listen respectfully, think about what was being presented, and enter into the discussion. Compare this example with the learning environment surrounding most youth sports activities. In which one will children be more likely to learn?

Essential Ingredients for the Warm-Up

In order to create the positive environment necessary for an effective Warm-Up meeting, a number of ingredients need to be in place. The players need to be able to focus their attention, free from undue distractions. They need to feel safe and comfortable in joining their coach and teammates in discussing relevant and sometimes difficult issues and concerns. They need to feel that this time spent preparing for the game or practice is meaningful and important, that it sets the stage for the upcoming activity.

The following items are essential ingredients for an effective Warm-Up session.

- **Design Your Physical Space**

  The first step in creating your sports classroom is to think about your physical environment. Is there a place to gather that is relatively free from outside distractions? In order for the players to be able to concentrate on the topics at hand (and remember, we're dealing with children here, who need little to distract them anyway) a setting as free from distractions as possible is vital.

  Along with this distraction-free space, take a look at how your sports classroom is set up. How do you organize your equipment? Hats, gloves, and balls strewn all around implies acceptance of a disorganized atmosphere. Come up with systems for keeping equipment, both team and personal, in its place.

- **Position Yourself**

  Once you have a place to conduct the Warm-Up, you need to consider how to position yourself in relation to your group. Think about having to always look up—literally—to see the person speaking to you. An uncomfortable position in a number of respects.

  The best arrangement for conducting the Warm-Up is with the players sitting or kneeling, gathered in a semicircle facing the coach, who is also sitting or kneeling. This puts you in front of the players, where they can all easily see and directly interact both with you and their teammates. It brings you down eye level, and you are positioned as one of the group. This close proximity with your young players creates a relaxed, comfortable environment.

- **Focus the Players' Attention**

  Once coach Parent gathered the team, how did he gain the attention of his players? How did he get them to focus? Coach Parent did not have to yell. No one, including kids, likes being yelled at. Effective coaches use simple organizing tools to shape their environment and get their players' attention.

Coach Parent gradually brought the kids to focus on the meeting. He asked Charlie to round up the others. When he raised his hand, Gordon raised his, and the other players followed. Coach Parent had introduced the "hand tool" earlier to symbolize silence and time to listen to the speaker. Few words were spoken and no one had to shout to be heard.

Young children respond quickly to adults who calmly but confidently teach and direct. Coach Parent's caring but firm approach allows children to shift gradually from what they were thinking about—maybe something as silly as slapping the back of the kid sitting next to them—to focusing on the Warm-Up meeting.

- **Rules of Conduct**

Every good classroom has rules of conduct intended to foster a positive learning atmosphere. Raising your hand before speaking, not interrupting, and listening to others are some important rules under which your sports classroom will thrive.

Use the Full Value Contract to establish the basis of how players treat each other. This simple agreement, made by all the members of your team, asks that each player will fully value themselves, others, and the game. It also asks that all team members, coaches included, work together toward stated goals, both individual and team oriented. The Full Value Contract will provide you and your players with a foundation for how your players conduct themselves and treat each other.

Establishing Rules of Behavior— Using the Full Value Contract

While most coaches of youth sports teams may agree that they would like to develop a team whose players trust and value themselves, the team process, other players, and coaches, few know how to take concrete steps toward creating such an atmosphere. How can you, right from the beginning of the season, create a climate that fosters this type of team unity and respect?

Project Adventure, the publisher of this book, uses a simple but comprehensive way to help establish such a climate. The Full Value Contract (FVC) is an agreement among players, coaches, and even parents that provides a mechanism for you to actively address the five PLUS values. Simply put, the FVC provides the following principles or rules:

- Team members will value and respect themselves.
- Team members will value and respect the team and the game.
- Team members will value and respect each other and the coach.
- Team members will set and work toward team and individual goals.

If you think that the children on your team may not fully understand the concepts of valuing and respecting, try using the following simplified version that Project Adventure often uses with younger children:

- Play Hard
- Play Safe
- Play Fair

However you explain it, introduce the concepts of the Full Value Contract right at the beginning of the season. Spend the first few Warm-Up meetings before practices discussing the five PLUS values. You can then introduce the FVC and discuss what a contract is and why it is important that the team agree to some basic principles of behavior. Continue this process by establishing specific rules of behavior, like *no put downs*, and consequences for infractions. (See Chapter Eight for more on developing rules and consequences.)

Get creative and have the children write the contract on a ball or bat. Each player can then sign their name to this team icon, making a concrete reminder of what they have agreed to. Or create a team contract, a copy of which each player signs and keeps.

Asking the children to agree to a contract that contains rules for specific, observable behaviors gives you a handy and quickly understood tool. "Is that behavior part of what you agreed to in our contract?" is usually all that is needed to remind players of how they should be behaving.

As simple as the above rules are, they work. Every dilemma or conflict that I can think of can be resolved by returning to the basic tenets of the Full Value Contract and asking an individual or the group whether they are adhering to it.

- **Promote Dialogue**

  Children learn by watching, listening, and having the opportunity to test their ideas with others. Too often, the coach wants to control the situation and do all the talking. Adults often feel they will lose control if they empower children to enter into the discussion. But interactive dialogue and empowerment do not mean abdication of control.

  The fact is, if we want sports to promote overall development and teach positive values, then we need to empower our children to think and engage in dialogue. Cognitive developmental psychology indicates that active dialogue encourages children to think critically, which in turn promotes intellectual development. Asking your players what they think about shifting the defense in the second half, for example, encourages intellectual growth. (Chapter Seven details using dialogue as a learning tool.)

- **Agenda**

  Having a clear and stated purpose for your Warm-Up will help you focus and keep the discussion on track. Children will often go off on their own tangents. You need to tactfully redirect the discussion if it goes too far astray from your stated agenda. This is especially important if one child criticizes another for making a mistake. Don't let the Warm-Up become a gripe session. Instead, remind them of their Full Value Contract and tell children that if they have a serious concern, they should talk to you alone.

  Use this time for discussing important issues, like a recent loss or some incident that has your players talking; for setting and revisiting team and individual goals; restating team rules; for explaining the skills you will be concentrating on in the practice; for outlining strategy for an upcoming game. But remember, once you get the discussion going, let them do the talking.

- **Be a Teacher**

  Along with learning sports skills like bunting and fielding, children need opportunities to explore and practice life skills and values. You, as the coach, are a teacher with many opportunities to present valuable lessons and the responsibility to structure an environment in which children feel emotionally and physically safe. You also need to develop the intellectual as well as the physical capabilities of your players.

Warm-Up Session Tools

The above list provides the basic ingredients for running a Warm-Up meeting. There are a number of additional tools you can use. The following strategies will help create an effective Warm-Up.

- **Raise Hand to Symbolize Silence and Attention**

   The players respond to the coach's hand up by putting their own hands up. "When your hand goes up, your mouth goes shut." One of the first tools a team can adopt is raising a hand to symbolize that it is time to listen. Children enjoy this tool because it quiets the team at a time when they are unable to do so on their own, and the coach doesn't have to yell to get their attention.

   The hand up gesture symbolically changes the culture of the environment. This simple tool takes very little time to implement; within one or two practices it will become an excellent means to establish order and get the kids attention. The coach promotes respectful leadership in this case because he is involving the children to help establish quiet.

- **Create a Team Rules Ball**

   Every team needs rules to organize their goals and set standards of behavior. Coach Parent begins the season by helping the children create a Team Rules Ball that outlines the basic rules of the team in observable and measurable behaviors. One rule, for example, might be that players will respect others when they are talking. This rule is easy to recognize, understand, follow, and measure. The players will begin to call each other on their own when they see a rule being broken.

Tip: Have a different child be responsible for bringing the Rules Ball to practices and games each week.

A major value of the Team Rules Ball is that the players make it and then help enforce it. Having the players create their own team rules lets the kids know that they are part of the process and encourages thinking. The Team Rules Ball should be present when the team conducts the Warm-Up and Cool-Down sessions. You can also create a sheet with team rules on it for players to hang up at home. This has the advantage of informing parents of the rules your team has developed.

- **Clarify the Issues Being Discussed**

To head off any confusion and misinformation, Coach Parent begins each meeting by describing the issues and goals to be discussed. It is important that the team understand exactly what the goals of each Warm-Up session are. The coach's role is to frame the learning experience. This introduction by the coach should be followed by questions from the players that clarify the goals or challenges.

- **Sum Up the Previous Point**

Everyone likes to jump in with what they have to say. Oftentimes players do not listen to what is being said because they are concentrating on what they will say next. One way to help children listen is to make them responsible for summing up, to the satisfaction of the previous speaker, what was said, before stating their own view. The players must listen to and understand each other's point of view. This helps them hold two contrary points of view while moving toward a solution that considers both responses. (This process can be tedious and is not always necessary, especially if the children are sticking to the problem being discussed.)

- **Keep the Players Engaged**

  One way to keep players engaged is to ask open-ended questions. When first introducing the value of fair play, Coach Parent asks the players to define what they think fair play means. He then uses their remarks to ask more questions to expand their thinking and provide broader examples.

  The questions you ask, and how you ask them, will influence the answers the players offer. For example, if you use the very general question "What did you guys think of the game?" to a team of eight-year-olds, the responses will likely be equally general. That may be all right, but sometimes you want your players to think about specific areas. This requires questions that ask for specific information, focusing the players' attention on the issues at hand.

  Just as when you designed your physical space to capture your players attention and minimize distractions, when you ask questions you need to direct your players' attention toward the desired topic. With a little practice, you will come up with questions that work well for you and your team.

Topics to Address

Go into each Warm-Up session with a clear idea of what you want to accomplish. Having this in mind will help the kids think about the topics at hand and keep irrelevant discussions and comments to a minimum.

There are two types of topics to discuss: Proactive topics are those you introduce for the purpose of teaching skills such bunting or values such as teamwork and perseverance. Reactive topics arise when the coach and the team are presented with an issue that came up during a previous game or practice. Reactive topics include incidents like a tough loss, a blatant rules infraction, or any thing else that has the players talking and concerned.

The following will help you outline an approach to your Warm-Up session that focuses on topics you want to address.

- **Opening the Session**

  Briefly open each Warm-Up with a description of what you want to accomplish during the session. Also ask if anyone has another

TEAM RULES
1. respect equipment.
2. respect each other and other teams.
3. listen to coach.
4. play fair and follow rules!

issue they want to bring up, but be prepared to direct the discussion of their issue back to the team. Set the stage for what you want the players to be thinking about.

- **Rules of the Team**

    One of the first topics to discuss at Warm-Up meetings are the team rules. Children love to make rules, and the ones they come up with are usually the ones a team needs to be happy and successful. Revisiting the rules periodically or pointing out infractions helps remind the team of their importance.

- **Team Goals**

    Every Warm-Up session should include two or three goals that the players can understand and execute. Coach Parent always makes sure to combine sports skills, such as "hitting the cutoff person" with learning values such as responsibility. When discussing responsibility, he breaks the concept into behaviors the players can see and understand, such as coming to practice on time and helping organize equipment. (See Chapter Eight for more on goal setting.)

- **Individual Goals**

  This is a good time to have the children set individual goals. You don't need to let all the players recite their goals; you'll never get out of the Warm-Up. Tell them that you will be going around during practice or at the game asking each of them what their individual goal is and how they are doing working towards it.

- **Skills**

  Outline the skills the children will be working on during an upcoming practice. You have their attention so it's a good time to at least outline the skills they will be practicing. You can also relate these skills to team or individual goals.

- **Game Strategies**

  A brief Warm-Up, conducted just before a game, will be the last chance you'll have to talk to your team before they take the field. You can restate goals they should be working on and strategies discussed at practice.

- **Closing**

  Don't let your Warm-Ups straggle off without a sense of closure. End each one with some sort of team cheer, or at least an enthusiastic "Let's play a good game!" A cheer that becomes part of the team culture is an effective way to bring all the players together and feel part of their team.

Summary

The Warm-Up session is about creating an atmosphere that is conducive to positive learning. These few minutes before practices and games become part of the team culture. The Warm-Up helps the players transition away from what they have been doing and focus on the coming activity. It is also a critical piece in establishing the environment you want to create for your team, where the kids are part of the process and feel safe and comfortable in discussing issues of importance to them as individuals and to the team.

By creating a time and place where your young athletes can discuss these topics in a positive, supportive atmosphere, you are providing opportunities for their intellectual development and promoting dialogue skills and critical thinking.

CHAPTER FOUR

The Activity

One of Coach Goodsport's learning goals is to ensure that her athletes develop positive attitudes toward rules, team play, teammates, winning, and losing. She has made these values clear by setting specific goals at the beginning of the season. Her Warm-Up sessions often revisit the team's rules and values to check in on how the children feel they are doing. However, Coach Goodsport knows that setting a goal is only the first step in encouraging good athletes and good people. Yesterday's soccer game provided a natural teachable moment, a learning opportunity recognized by both coach and players.

Tommy Too-Cool scored three goals in the final quarter of a winning effort. While the players were shaking hands, Tommy was acting cocky and boasting about how great he is. He was about to take off when Coach Goodsport called the team together for a Cool-Down session. Coach Goodsport asked the team to sum up some of the important aspects of the game. Comments like "We played awesome," "We kicked butt," and "we played as a team," were the most common responses. Coach Goodsport agreed but pointed out that the team needed to work on "listening." The team then set goals for the next practice.

As the team left, Coach Goodsport took Tommy aside and spoke to him about his comments and actions. She agreed that he was a good player but pointed out that his attitude about himself and others was not positive and was preventing him from improving as a player and a person. She said that he does not have to brag about his accomplishments, because others will notice them. Furthermore, others might begin to resent players who brag a lot. More important, there may be a time when he won't be a star and will have to adjust to be more of a team player. Coach Goodsport asked if this made sense, and Tommy said it did, and that he would work on his attitude. Coach Goodsport said he was a good player and she was excited about what he had learned.

Tommy didn't like what he had heard, but said that he would try harder because he wants to be liked by his peers, and he likes being on the team. Tommy believes that Coach Goodsport treats everyone fairly and that she would have done the same to anyone else on the team. She is consistent, and she spoke with him alone, not in front of the other children.

❖

Throughout this book I suggest that, if sports are to develop important skills and values, we need to create an environment where teaching and learning can occur easily and naturally. Specifically, we focus on the goals of teamwork, respect, responsibility, fair play, and perseverance. The Warm-Up sessions provide you with the first step in creating an active learning environment in which to teach these values. Once the Warm-Up session ends and the Activity phase of the PLUS Learning Cycle begins, we are presented with perhaps the most powerful opportunities for sports to develop life skills and positive values.

"Experience is not what happens to you; it is what you do with what happens to you."

—Aldous Huxley

The Value and Power of Experience

In and of itself, the Activity is just that, an activity. But considering the above quote, and the notion that experience is the best teacher, it takes only a simple twist of thought to recognize that sports activity becomes truly meaningful, experiences truly capable of teaching important life lessons, when we make a conscious decision to do something with the experiences the activity offers.

It is in the Activity phase of the PLUS Learning Cycle that the players practice their skills and goals. If the coach and team have done a good job of outlining the team's core values, goals, and rules in *observable* behaviors, then the process of recognizing those instances during the activity when the values, goals, or rules are either broken or followed will be less random and more conscious. For example, the coach and team can observe whether the equipment is lined up, who initiated responsibility, and who did not help.

There are many examples of teachable moments that occur in youth sports activities and relate to the five PLUS core values The purpose of this chapter will be to focus on *how* to recognize and then *what to do* with these teach-able moments you are presented with. Think about how Coach Goodsport handled the following situation that occurred during soccer practice.

> Coach Goodsport needs to split the team up into two sides to practice a drill. The Blue team begins to form a line on one side, the Orange team on the other. Blue team members Tommy Too-Cool and Slam-Dunk Sam start to tell the Orange team that they are better and they are going to "kick their butts." The children on the Orange team don't pay much attention to the remarks, realizing the two boys are out of line.
>
> Coach Goodsport hears the remarks but continues to organize the children and asks the teams to begin. She then calls the two boys off to the side and explains to them why their remarks are disruptive to practice. She asks them to think about what they could have done to make the team-choosing process go more smoothly. She tells them that they can talk to the team and share their suggestions after the game. She closes by saying that they have a lot to offer and she enjoys having them on the team.

There are a number of ways that this situation could have been dealt with. Coach Goodsport chose to address the issue, allowing the practice to con-tinue but at the same time providing an opportunity for the boys to learn that their actions did not support their team's values of teamwork and respect. Equally important, the entire incident was handled in a quiet, effective, and positive manner; the boys were not ridiculed in front of their teammates for their behavior.

Teachable moments can occur at any time and without warning. No matter where you find yourself within the PLUS Learning Cycle, you need to remem-ber and employ some basic tools. For example, when engaged in the process of teaching and learning, you should also be concerned with the design of your surrounding sports classroom; are there distractions? If you are address-ing an issue with a single player, have you removed yourself from the rest of the group? Are you employing the rules of interactive dialogue, asking the right questions, and providing opportunities for the players to respond?

In general, all the ingredients and tools, such as interactive dialogue (see Chapter Seven), listening, and eye contact that make for an effective Warm-Up should also be used when dealing with teachable moments. If you have cre-ated a climate within which your athletes know they will be treated with re-spect and caring, then addressing issues with individuals, groups of players, or the entire team will not be difficult. The atmosphere of trust and safety you are building will ensure that players listen to you, understand, discuss, and work to change their behavior.

Tips for Recognizing Teachable Moments

The first step in using teachable moments is recognizing them when they occur. Sports provide numerous opportunities to teach values, but in order for positive learning to take place, the teachable moments must be recognized. Too often these moments are missed, ignored, or handled ineffectively.

Bringing Values to Life

In order to make values come to life and have meaning for children, they must be made *observable*, *measurable*, and *understandable*. Words like teamwork, responsibility, and respect are simply too abstract for most children to understand. They need to be acted out in observable behaviors. While asking your players to bring their equipment to every practice may not seem like an example of teamwork, it presents a concrete behavior that can be observed and understood. "If you don't bring your equipment, you won't be able to practice the drills with the rest of the team and you won't be ready for the game on Saturday. If you are not as prepared as you should be, you can't fully contribute to the team." Here is a behavior that can be understood by the children; pointed out and reinforced by the coach.

Using Levels to Measure Core Values

The leader-to-detractor scale attaches specific behaviors to the five core values, providing a tool to measure your teams progress in following them. The scale can be discussed with the children as the season begins and reinforced during regular Warm-Up and Cool-Down meetings. One way to use it, especially with younger children, is to introduce one value per week at practice. This gives the kids a chance to discuss each one and begin to learn what it means before going on to another.

The scale provides five levels on which both general and specific behaviors can fall. For example, a child who hurts someone's feelings is a detractor in relation to the value of respect. On the positive side, a child who reminds a teammate to bring his equipment to practice is demonstrating concern for others and is at the leader end of the scale. A person who neither detracts nor actively contributes but only observes is at level two.

This scale is not intended to be a report card; it is simply another tool to help you provide meaning to the core values. With a common language and commonly understood levels of behavior, your players will be in a better position to engage in meaningful dialogue. This in turn helps children begin to transfer the lessons learned in their sports experience to other situations away from the playing field—at school or at home.

PLUS Themes in Action

With the help of the scales, behaviors and actions can be discussed with a child in more understandable ways. When both the coach and the child recognize where a behavior falls on the PLUS scale, the coach and child can then set goals for the child to move up the scale by changing specific behaviors.

Teamwork

Sports provide opportunities for players with different backgrounds and interests to relate to one another as members of the same team. Teamwork is an important life skill.

Levels of Teamwork

> **5.0** Understands role as a contributing team member plus models the value of teamwork.
>
> **4.0** Understands role as a member of team and seeks opportunities to display teamwork.
>
> **3.0** Understands role as a member of a team with common goals but displays little proactive teamwork.
>
> **2.0** Engages in teamwork only when directed and to promote self-interests.
>
> **1.0** Detracts from team. No regard for teammates. "One-person team," hogs the ball.

Respect

Respect is a fundamental value that, along with responsibility, forms the basis of the moral fabric for any family, team, or community. Respect for self and others requires that we treat all forms of life as inherently special. From respect stem many other values, such as compassion, courtesy, honesty, respect for authority, and respect for differences in ability, race, culture, and gender.

Levels of Respect

5.0 Communicates and displays through actions deep concern and caring for the person's worth as a human. Commits to enabling the other person's growth.

4.0 Communicates caring and concern for the other person. Makes others feel valued as individuals.

3.0 Expression of minimal acknowledgment, regard, or concern for the person's feelings, experience, or potential.

2.0 No thought for the feelings, experience, and potential of the other person.

1.0 Negative regard. Lack of respect, hurts others' feelings.

Responsibility

Responsibility is the active side of respect and calls for acting upon one's moral values. Responsibility is the glue that holds a team, family, or community together. It is one thing to respect your teammate and it is another to take the responsibility to show that respect in tangible actions. Responsibility is also the moral extension of caring. It is the carrying out of our obligation to someone or to something (such as the team) greater than ourselves. A sense of responsibility to oneself, to a friend, to a coach, teacher, or parent, to a class, family, or team forms a base for our actions.

Levels of Responsibility

5.0 Takes an active role in being accountable to the team plus actively models responsibility for others.

4.0 Understands role in situations plus seeks opportunities to be responsible.

3.0 Understands what it means to be responsible but takes no active role.

2.0 Assumes responsibility/accountability when confronted directly.

1.0 Avoids becoming responsible/accountable. "Here it comes, there I go."

Fair Play

Understanding how our actions and our role as a team member impact others is an important moral value. Understanding issues of fairness in regards to rules, relationships, and distribution of playing time is an essential skill in life. Organized sports, with their rules and opportunities to share with people of similar and different backgrounds, provide a natural medium to model and teach notions of fair play.

Levels of Fair Play

5.0 Understands role as leader in issues of fairness plus models and teaches others the idea of fairness.

4.0 Understands role in regard to fairness and seeks opportunities to display fairness.

3.0 Understands the purpose of fairness in relation to situation of team but does not actively display examples of fair play.

2.0 Complies with rules and equity only if has to. "I share playing time because I have to."

1.0 Negative regard for fairness, rules, and equity. Criticizes and resists sharing playing time.

Perseverance

It is easy to be excited and motivated when things are going your way. The ability to keep trying, to give one's best in spite of setbacks, disappointments, and opposition is an important ingredient of success. In the long run, perseverance will often win out over talent.

Levels of Perseverance

5.0 Shows a positive attitude especially when the team is losing. Encourages others to keep working their hardest.

4.0 Understands that persevering and keeping motivated is an important goal. Keeps trying and works hard.

3.0 Understands and accepts the concept of perseverance but gets discouraged when difficulties arise.

2.0 Perseveres and works hard only when directly confronted by coaches and teammates.

1.0 Avoids working hard. Gives up easily and is vocal in complaints when things are not going his way.

Addressing Teachable Moments

Just as there are ingredients that help create a positive environment for the Warm-Up session, there are ingredients that help deal with teachable moments in a positive and productive manner.

- **Assess the Situation**

    Ask the following questions:

    What is the real problem? Why is it a problem?

    Does the situation require an immediate response or should it wait for the next Cool-Down or Warm-Up?

    Should the issue be handled publicly or privately?

    Is it a personal or a team issue?

    What needs to be done to solve the problem?

    How are the children involved feeling?

    Am I being a positive role model?

- **Refer to the Full Value Contract**

  Sometimes simply taking a child aside and reminding them of their agreement to the FVC is enough to make the child aware that their behavior is not in keeping with what they agreed to. If the behavior continues, then move on to the leader-to-detractor scale and set specific goals with the child.

- **Use the Leader-to-Detractor Scale**

  Where does the observed behavior fall within the scale? Explain to the child or children how their behavior is not in keeping with a specific value. Explain how they can change their behavior to move up the scale. This is also a good time to set goals with the child, making sure that they understand in behavioral terms just what they need to do. Observe the child over time and discuss their progress toward their goal. (See Chapter Eight for more on goal setting.)

- **Focus on the Behavior, Not the Person**

  Discuss the behavior, not the child. For example, Tommy Too-Cool may engage in poor sportsmanship, but he is not a bad kid. Always try to make clear to your players that you are disappointed in their actions but not in them as people. Try to end these discussions with something positive about their personality. "Tommy, I was really happy to see you apologize to the ref the other day. I am proud of you for that."

- **Use Relationship Skills**

  Children are more impressed with how we treat them than with what we say. If you want to be successful with your team, follow the guidelines for building healthy relationships (see Chapter Six). Always give a child the opportunity to offer an explanation. Discuss, don't preach or lecture.

- **Return to Your Philosophy and Values**

  Whenever you are engaged with your players, continuously return to the basic values of your team. Issues that need to be addressed will be easier to resolve if your players understand that the values players, parents, and coaches have agreed on are important.

Over time, both you and your team will come to understand the process for recognizing and then addressing teachable moments. This process will quickly become part of your team's culture, and the kids themselves will begin to recognize rule infractions and times when stated team values are not being met. It is critical that you set the tone for the ways that teachable moments are dealt with. Private conversations rather than public scoldings, for example, ensure an atmosphere of trust and respect, in which real learning can take place, and where even the most difficult issues can be addressed openly and honestly.

Summary

The Activity phase is what it is all about—practicing skills and playing the game. Kids dream about walking up to bat in the bottom of the ninth, sinking a three-pointer at the buzzer, and scoring the winning goal. During the Activity phase emotions are high...it is the time the kids have been waiting for. During this phase of the PLUS Learning Cycle, the team is presented with opportunities to put their skills, goals, and values into practice. Once the Activity begins, the learning process becomes real and observable. The kids are no longer just talking about it, they are doing it! If a child strikes out, throws the bat, and swears on her way back to the bench the coaches and players have actual behaviors and emotions to discuss. But teachable moments take on value only when recognized and addressed in a way that includes the learning principles outlined throughout this book.

CHAPTER FIVE

The Cool-Down

"Tough game, guys...looks like we need to practice and get some new umps. Practice next Thursday night—don't be late! Teresa, tell your brother to bring his Easton bat to practice."

Coach Neophyte's team, the Bristol Rockets, just lost a close game to the Cougars, and he is not pleased. The players grudgingly shake hands with the Cougars and begin to drift off the field. Mr. and Mrs. Pressure are angry at the umpire because they feel he missed a close call that won the game for the Cougars. Dr. and Dr. Competitive are yelling from the opposite sides of the field as their son, Noah, hangs his head and walks toward his mother's new car. He pitches his glove through the back window. The Rockets are experiencing a lot of emotions—for the most part these emotions are not happy ones.

Coach Neophyte and the Rockets represent a fairly typical coach and team responding to a fairly typical youth sports game. They also represent the typical manner in which most games end. In the case of the Rockets, a number of feelings and teachable moments are left unaddressed. Who will talk to Noah? What will his parents, Dr. and Dr. Competitve, tell him? What values will they reinforce? What will Mr. and Mrs. Pressure teach Timid Teresa about blaming the umpire? What will she learn about taking responsibility for her actions?

Will they subtly teach her that blaming authority is a positive way to deal with frustration? In the case of the Rockets, the sports experience and all the potential teachable moments are left to chance.

On the other side of the field a more conscious type of learning is under way. During the Warm-Up session, Coach Parent had introduced a number of important goals that were then practiced during the game. He knows that his players observed a lot of unsportsmanlike behavior and that they watched

how Coach Neophyte reacted. The Cougars have a lot of emotions that need sorting out, and a number of potential learning opportunities to address. Coach Parent understands that his role is to facilitate and frame the learning process. The Cool-Down is an excellent forum to debrief all that has happened.

> The atmosphere feels good on the Cougars' side of the field. Part of the positive atmosphere is due to the close win, but the truth is the Cougars' side of the field always seems positive. Coach Parent does not have to yell or do much to gather his team for their post-game meeting. The Cougars look forward to their Cool-Down sessions, because they get to talk about the game and discuss the goals set during the Warm-Up.
>
> "Nice game, team," Coach Parent shares with a smile. "What do you think?"
>
> "We were awesome! We hit better than we usually do," says Tommy.
>
> "I think we came together as a team in the last two innings," Gordon adds.
>
> "What about the goals we set in the Warm-Up session? Can anyone please define them and share with us how well we did?"
>
> "We should make good throws to the cutoff person."
>
> "How did we do?"
>
> "We only missed two."
>
> "Can anyone remember our other team goals?" asks Coach Parent.
>
> To everyone's surprise, Tommy remembers that responsibility was a team goal. Coach Parent comments that he saw Tommy line up the bats during the fourth inning. Suddenly Ken says he's thought of another way team members can "do responsible acts."
>
> "When the game is over we can help put the equipment away and carry it to Coach's car. He has to do it all himself now."
>
> "That's a great idea!" said Coach Parent. "Next practice is on Tuesday and we have a game on Thursday night. I want us to think of other acts of teamwork we can do. I also want to introduce the right way to do sacrifice bunts. During our Warm-Up before practice on Tuesday, we will discuss different ways we can be better team members. It would be fun for you guys to think about how you can 'do teamwork' before our Tuesday practice. Great game today. Does anyone have anything to say?"
>
> "Yeah, we are awesome!"

Why The Cool-Down Session?

If we want children to learn positive character values from their early sports experiences, we must take advantage of learning opportunities as they present themselves. When the Activity portion of the PLUS Learning Cycle ends, the children's emotions are charged. Feelings are bubbling at the surface. The Cool-Down phase possesses unique learning opportunities for a number of reasons. First, directly after the Activity players can easily see the direct connections between values and behavior, between goals and performance. The children want to talk, sorting through the strong emotions they are experiencing. Waiting for a later day would allow these emotions to fade and the players may forget how the experience felt at the time. Providing an immediate opportunity to deal with their emotions helps purposeful learning. At no other time in the youth sports experience are the connections so fresh and immediate.

Second, by addressing right away the issues that arise during the Activity, especially potentially difficult ones that may have children confused, angry, or hurt you can diffuse a lot of those feelings rather than allowing them to continue to trouble the kids. The children may be looking for an adult who they respect and feel comfortable talking with to sort out these confusing feelings. You also have an opportunity to discuss with the players as a group any incident that may be grounds for the rumor mill.

Third, the Cool-Down Session offers a time to evaluate the team's performance and effort in relation to their goals. Team goals set during the Warm-Up session can be discussed. The Cool-Down also provides coaches and players with an opportunity to set new goals for the next practice.

Fourth, the Cool-Down brings a sense of closure to the Activity phase of the cycle. Rather than straggling off the field after practice or a game with questions or feelings left unresolved, your players will be able to bring a sense of completeness to the Activity and recognize that this portion of the sports experience is now over. It brings the team full circle, poised for the cycle to begin again at the next Warm-Up. The Cool-Down also brings up issues for the players to discuss with their parents.

The Cool-Down session needs many of the same ingredients that go into a well-constructed Warm-Up. There is, however, one additional ingredient that deserves special attention. Used extensively by Project Adventure in all their group work, the debrief or processing portion of the Cool-Down is perhaps the key to ensure that learning takes place and that children begin to understand how their sports experiences can be directly related to life away from the playing field.

"Happy children are not those without problems or disappointments. Happy children are those with the abilities to deal with problems or disappointments."

Processing the Experience

Processing the experience of the Activity with your players is not difficult, nor does it need a lot of time. But learning how processing works, how to use it, and what to expect can matter a great deal for what your team learns from its experience.

If you begin your Cool-Down with a question like "How do you feel about the game?" you will likely get general or vague responses—"bad," "awesome," "great." Too often, we tend to jump right into the heart of the matter—how do you *feel?* Your kids may not be sure of how they are feeling. Maybe they won but are feeling bad because the other team made disrespectful remarks to them in the congratulating line. Rather than jumping right into a discussion, especially if there may be difficult topics to address, you need to ease into it. Give the kids a chance to focus on small pieces before you ask them to think about the experience as a whole.

A good way to do this is by following a sequence of questions:

What? So What? Now What?

What?

The best place to begin is to first get clear, for yourself and the kids, *What* happened. What did we do well? Did we achieve our goals? Did we practice our values? A good technique to get a discussion started and to involve everyone is to use a go-around exercise. To do this, have everyone provide a one- or two-word response, or short descriptive sentence about what happened. This puts less pressure on individuals and gives you a quick read on their attitude. If there is an issue you want to bring up that they have missed, put yourself into the go-around and put your issue out to the group that way.

These *What* questions and responses lead into interpretation and discussion of different views and feelings. They also raise the children's awareness of issues and behaviors to be maintained or changed. *What* questions give you a powerful tool to move the discussion in the direction you want it to go. You can move on to the next phase at any time and return to more *Whats* around the experience later on.

So What?

The next phase of the processing sequence is the *So What*? It is here that you begin asking the children to become more abstract in their thinking. In the *So What* you can ask your players why you have rules for the team in the first place and why are they important; why should you act respectfully toward others; and what it means to work toward goals and achieve them.

You can further challenge children's thinking by asking them why their experiences are important. How are these experiences useful beyond the playing field? Is what we are talking about here useful in school? At home? This is a good intellectual exercise and helps in the development of critical thinking skills, teaching children how to generalize from one experience to another.

Now What?

This is a good way to bring the Cool-Down to closure and complete the PLUS Learning Cycle. We know what we did, and we have asked ourselves the importance of what happened. But now what do we do with these lessons? *Now What* questions ask the children to think about their experience in a broader context. "How can what we have learned help us in our next game or practice? How can what we learned be applied to situations in school, with friends, with our families?" This furthers the intellectual exercise and leaves the team with things to think about until their next activity.

Ingredients of the Cool-Down

Although the Cool-Down session represents a distinct part of the PLUS Learning Cycle, the same teaching and learning principles and tools that make for an effective Warm-Up need to be employed.

Create a Positive Learning Climate

The need to create a positive learning environment is continuous; that is, it does not begin during the Warm-Up and end or change into something else during the game. In fact, the type of learning environment we create begins when we first meet with our players at the beginning of the season. As you move into the different phases of the Learning Cycle, the environment is a continuation of what you have already created.

Focus the Team

Once the game has ended, there are lots of potential distractions that can interfere with a positive learning environment. Kids can be excited or upset. Parents are beginning to crowd around. The equipment is usually strewn all over and mom and dad want to go home. Amidst this chaos the coach needs to focus the team both physically and socially in a way similar to the Warm-Up session. However, given the distractions the coach may need to play a more active role.

Do your best to diminish these distractions. Holding the Cool-Down out by the pitcher's mound or a tree in left field will work well. Once you do this a couple of times, it will become a ritual, part of your team's culture, and the players will know where they need to go and what they need to do. Over time the parents will understand that the Cool-Down session is an important phase of the Learning Cycle.

As in the Warm-Up, arrange your players so that they either sit or kneel, facing away from their parents and toward you. Get their attention and start the discussion. Use the processing techniques to get the discussion going but then do as little talking as possible.

Create a Quiet Focus

Because the players will be emotionally and physically worked up from the game, the coach needs to allow for a little quiet focus before beginning the debriefing process. This is distinctly different from the Warm-Up. The best way to create a quiet focus is to model it. Allow the players to slowly gather around. Do not counter every noise, question, or remark with a response. You may want to give them a minute of free-flowing talk. Show through facial expressions and hand gestures that it is time to start the Cool-Down session. Gentle but directive hand movements with an occasional *shsssshh* will gradually soothe the situation and create a sense of quiet calm.

Cool-Down Session Tools

Your greatest tool in conducting an effective Cool-Down will be the processing techniques presented above. In addition, many of the same tools used in the Warm-Up session are effective in the Cool-Down. The one notable difference after the Activity will be in the behavior and attitudes of the players , especially after a game. They may behave quite differently depending on whether they won or lost.

Bring Your Team Rules Ball or Bat

Bringing the ball or bat with the team rules on it will give the players a concrete reminder of the rules they have developed and becomes an important part of the team's culture—part of who they are and what their team stands for.

Use the Hand-Raising Gesture

Just as it focuses the children for the Warm-Up discussion and quiets them down without your having to shout, the symbolic gesture of raising your hand will be equally effective in the Cool-Down.

Clarify the Issues

When necessary, restate and clarify issues the players are discussing to be sure that they all understand what is being discussed and why. Keep them focused on the relevant topics, but always try to let them do the talking.

Keep the Players Engaged

The processing questions and techniques will help ensure that all of the children will be engaged in the Cool-Down dialogue and everyone will have an opportunity to express their thoughts and feelings. Keeping all the players actively involved will help prevent them from tuning out and distracting others.

Topics to Address

You will likely have no trouble in finding enough topics to address during the Cool-Down. The biggest difficulty may be in deciding which items get attention. Remembering the discussion on recognizing teachable moments in the previous chapter should help you to focus in on some particularly important points. During Cool-Downs, especially post-game, the children will likely be quite eager to talk but may not always focus in on the learning opportunities that you have spotted. Using the processing techniques presented earlier in this chapter should help you direct your players to the teachable moments you have identified and want to discuss with them.

Revisit Goals

The Cool-Down session is the time to revisit goals set during previous Warm-Ups. The children have their performance and effort during the Activity they have just finished as immediate and observable measures. Goals should include both skills and values. Point to specific moments during the activity as examples.

Teachable Moments

The Cool-Down session provides a time to discuss learning opportunities you've identified during the game or practice.

Revisit Team Rules

While this can be part of addressing teachable moments, you may simply want to remind the kids of their rules, without pointing to any specific incident or infraction.

Positive Feedback on Values

This is a good opportunity to point out specific examples of players acting in ways that reinforce your team's stated values. Who was a leader or a contributor toward a value, and what was their behavior?

Set Goals for the Next Game or Practice

The final piece of the Cool-Down session is to set new goals for the next practice or game. This activity continues the PLUS Learning Cycle and provides the coach and team with a place to pick up where you left off. "Did we try to learn something new or get better at something you already know?" "Was it due to a lack of effort or because of the way the game went?" "Could we have worked harder or smarter?" "What do we want to set as goals for our next practice?"

Closure

A team cheer, a handshake, or some well-chosen, thoughtful words from the coach bring the Cool-Down to a close and can quickly become part of your team's culture. This also lets the kids know that their sport experience, for this time and day, is now complete.

Summary

The Cool-Down phase offers distinct learning opportunities and completes the PLUS Learning Cycle. The post-game meeting provides the coach and players with the opportunity to revisit team goals set during the Warm-Up, debrief the team's performance, discuss important incidents and issues, help the children sort out confusing feelings, and set new goals for the next game and practice.

As we all have witnessed, most youth sports games end with a quick huddle followed by the teams shaking hands. The coach yells a few directives: "Be at the field by 5:15 next Tuesday!" as the players disperse and head to their parents' cars. The parents are seldom equipped with an understanding of what questions to ask or how to work through their child's feelings. The Cool-Down offers an organized and consistent process to encourage positive learning and the transference of that learning to general life situations.

This simple yet important time holds the potential to transform our children's sports experiences into a time to learn valuable character-building skills.

The Second Quarter

How Children Learn

Taken together, Role Modeling, Dialogue, and Rewards and Consequences represent three ways children can learn from participating in organized sports. These three important *principles of learning* are understood and defined by educational psychology.

1. The *Social Learning Theory* states people learn through interacting and observing others.

2. The *Cognitive-Developmental Learning Theory* states that people learn through active dialogue about important issues.

3. The *Behavioral Learning Theory* suggests that people learn through rewards and consequences.

Understanding how children learn within sports environments allows us to better shape the environment and create positive sports experiences.

CHAPTER SIX

Learning Through Modeling and Relationships

A few years back there was a TV commercial where a father and son were washing their car. The father picked up the soap and scrubbed the car. The five-year-old picked up the sponge and scrubbed the car. The father picked up the hose and rinsed the car. The son picked up the hose and rinsed the car, just like his dad. The father reached for a pack of cigarettes, and the young child reached for the cigarettes. The commercial asked, "WHAT ARE WE TEACHING OUR CHILDREN?" There were no words exchanged, only a child modeling his father.

Kids learn a lot by watching others. They watch how we treat one another. They watch what we say, what we do, what we wear. Young athletes watch their sports heroes on tv and buy the sneakers their favorite player wears. They also emulate the behavior of their professional idols when the ref makes a bad call. When the coach of a youth sports team yells at the refs or the players, the kids are watching and learning.

For young children, the coach often represents one of their first adult role models other than parents and teachers. The coach shares with the child the fun, excitement, and disappointment of competitive activities. As a coach, you have a responsibility for the safety, education, and development of all the players on your team. Successful coaches teach important life lessons about fairness and caring, about persevering in the face of obstacles. While it is important that you, as coach, develop your team values and rules of behavior, it is crucial that you go on to model them. It is the coach who translates the values of a program into reality.

---

*"When a teacher understands and truly cares,
a student will appear."*

— Jeffrey Pratt Beedy

The Power of a Coach

Research shows that a coach has more of an impact on the overall psychological development of the child than the sport itself does. This places enormous responsibility on a coach but offers abundant opportunities to influence a child's early sports experience. The coach is above all a role model and mentor. Unfortunately, not all coaches understand the importance of their position.

What type of role model are you?

- Do you say one thing yet do another?
- How do you act when your team loses?
- How do you interact with the umpires or refs and other coaches?
- What type of language do you use?
- Do you enforce team rules fairly and consistently?
- Do you treat players differently?
- Do you listen when your players ask questions?

Coach Neophyte states that everyone on the team will receive an equal amount of playing time—this is his rule. The players like Coach Neophyte because he is funny, played semipro ball, and has lots of parties for the team. When tournament time arrives, however, Coach Neophyte plays only the best players. Some of the youngsters are happy and others are sad, but all of them are learning something about fairness and about what some adults really value.

The sad part of this story is that, because the young players think Coach Neophyte is cool, he may have more influence over them than their teachers or parents do when it comes to learning about issues of respect and fairness. Young children are impressed by the fact that he played semipro ball and can still hit the ball hard. They also watch him swear, chew tobacco, and say one thing about playing time but then act differently.

Being a Positive Role Model

Have you ever asked yourself, "Why do I coach?" There will be many answers to this simple but important question. "Because I enjoyed the sport as a child." "Because my child is currently playing." "Because I want to give something to my community." "To get out of the house!"

Regardless of your motivations, knowing why you want to coach in the first place will help you examine your coaching style. In one way or another, your athletes will respond to any coaching style. You can leave their learning to chance, or you can be a role model who provides them with an atmosphere that offers opportunities to learn positive character values.

The following tips are some of the things you can do to ensure that you are a positive role model for your players.

Attitude—Kids are always watching. Be positive and conduct yourself in the way you would want your players to act. We hold up the mirror for our children's image of what is appropriate.

Show respect for all players—Children watch to see how we treat others. Always show respect, even when you are upset and even when someone makes a bad play or asks a question that seems silly. Discuss matters privately with players rather than embarrassing them in front of their teammates.

Be positive about losing—Although it is sometimes tough, you need to maintain a positive attitude when your team loses. Let the kids know that there are more important outcomes of any game than the final score. (Refer back to Chapter One for more on winning and losing.)

Be consistent with rules—Kids watch to see if we mean what we say. If we make a rule that states no swearing, then we must, without exception, address each infraction as it arises. Inconsistency will only teach children that rules can be bent for certain players. The value of fairness will become confused.

Don't argue with the refs or other coaches—One of the most common ways kids learn poor sportsmanship is by watching their coach argue or yell at the refs. Do, however, stick up for your players. If one of your players complains that rude remarks were made in the congratulating line by a player on another team, talk to the other coach and point out that your team values respectful behavior and has rules about such conduct. If you approach this in a positive way, opposing coaches will usually be glad you spoke with them.

Language—Very simply, use only the language you want your players to use. If you tell your team they need to be respectful to others but then swear at a player or a ref, you are modeling the wrong behaviors.

Don't expect more from your players than you are willing to offer— If you ask your players to be on time, then you need to be on time. If you ask your players to be positive in the face of obstacles, such as a losing season, then you must be able to do the same.

Admit mistakes—One of the hardest things for many adults is to admit when we are wrong—especially to children. However, admitting that we make mistakes is probably one of the strongest ways to model healthy values. Children like adults who are human. Let me share the following story.

> One winter I ordered a NordicTrak and received it in the mail. I hate to put machines together but I had no choice. My eight-year-old daughter wanted to help. Although I appreciated her interest, she was making an already unpleasant activity more difficult. I finally snapped at her in a way I never had before. She unhappily left the room and told her mother that I was "frustrated with the machine."
>
> A few minutes later she came back into the room and jumped up on the newly assembled machine. At the time I could not figure out how to tighten the strap on the skis. My eight-year-old pushed one of the computer buttons and said she had figured out the problem. I said, "No, that is not the way it works." But I soon realized that she was right and told her that I was sorry for my attitude and sorry I didn't believe her. I was wrong. I was amazed at her reply. She told me that she didn't think adults like to admit that they are wrong. More to the point, she felt that "big people" don't think they can learn anything from "little people." Well, I learned something that day about how children view adults. I learned a lesson about learning.

Take responsibility—Sometimes we blame the children for troubles that arise. "The kids are wild!" "I can't do anything; they won't listen." We've all heard and probably made comments like these. Granted, children do get out of hand at times, but the adult has to take responsibility for the success or failure of the relationship. The coach is responsible for the behavior of the group. The kids are not to blame for the coach's ineffectiveness. Always remember: the coach is the adult and the athlete is the child.

Understand what kids want and need from adults—To be truly effective with children, we need to understand how they develop as people and as athletes. Specifically, we must learn to understand what children need and want. One thing children need and want is guidance. We need to be effective both in teaching specific sports skills—baseball, soccer, tennis, basketball, etc.—and in our relationships with young people. It is simply not enough to be good at the sport. (See Section Four for information on children's development by age.)

> *"We do not believe in ourselves until someone*
> *reveals that deep inside us something is valuable, worth*
> *listening to, worthy of our trust, sacred to our touch.*
> *Once we believe in ourselves we can risk curiosity,*
> *wonder, spontaneous delight, or any*
> *experience that reveals the human spirit."*
>
> — *e.e. cummings*

Creating Positive Relationships

Healthy relationships form the foundation of any family, school, or team. Healthy relationships are the number one factor in a positive sports experience. How does an unfocused eight-year-old suddenly become internally motivated to try a new sport? Why does a once-shy sixth-grade girl suddenly want to play in the final quarter of a big game? The magic of personal growth always takes place within the context of a relationship.

Healthy relationships provide people with a safe place where they can grow. Relationships provide us with a context, a mirror of sorts, where we can test thoughts and feelings and receive feedback that helps us develop. Children need adults who can understand them, as well as teach skills. Children depend on adults to create environments that are safe and supportive for exploring and taking risks.

The following are some of the ingredients, many of which are especially important to children, in developing healthy relationships. As in a cake recipe, the order in which the ingredients are listed is significant, reflecting the developmental nature of the way healthy relationships are formed. For example, the adult who invests time early in the relationship understands the child better and will be in a better position later on to offer direction and discipline. The truly masterful coach understands the value of developing relationships through the following sequence.

Time

Time is at the top of the list because it is the most important, yet most often neglected. Do not overlook the aspect of time as simple-minded. Adults can easily forget the importance of time to young children, usually because there never seems to be enough of it. Often, just being there for your players is all it takes. Taking the time for a quiet word of encouragement or a pat on the back, or stopping what you are doing to focus momentarily on a player with a problem or concern, means a great deal to the children.

Don't rush your players through practice because *you* have a schedule that must be met. Try to put yourself on the same time schedule as the kids. This doesn't mean abdicating control or giving up a schedule entirely. It simply means tuning into the needs of the kids at the moment. Giving yourself to their schedule lets the kids work off distracting energy, which then helps them focus better on the skills you want to present.

Attention

Another easy-to-do that is also often overlooked. We all want attention, especially young children. Attention provides important elements to the relationship. Sometimes attention alone "heals" a sprained ankle or bruised elbow. An eye-to-eye "how are you doing" with a pat on the back can quickly change the feelings of an otherwise dejected strike-out victim. Attention carries the message of caring.

Listening

Listening contributes a number of valuable ingredients to the coach/athlete relationship. First, listening allows the adult to understand what the problem is. This may seem obvious, but sometimes we think we know what the child is going to say, only to find out later that the child is hurt because we were not really listening. Listening does not necessarily mean agreeing. *Listening means giving the child your undivided attention.*

Listening also allows the child to hear what he or she is thinking. Initially, listen to what the child is saying and then repeat it back for clarification *without any subjective judgment.* This "active listening" allows them to hear their own thoughts and, often, answer their own questions. Children may say things simply to get an adult's reaction. They may not even believe what they are saying. At other times, the child very much believes what he or she is saying and wants an objective opinion. In either case, the adult plays an important role as an active listener.

You may ask, "When do I find the time to simply listen?" Obviously, we cannot always give a child our undivided attention. At least acknowledge that the child has a concern and tell them that you will discuss the matter at a time when you can give them your full attention. It is often a matter of emphasis and balance. But you won't believe the mileage you will get out of this.

Understanding

One of the most important ingredients of an effective relationship with children is the ability to understand their feelings, thoughts, and issues. This cannot be over-emphasized. Does it mean that we always agree? Absolutely not! It is always important to remember that we are the adults and the child is the child. Being understanding does not necessarily mean agreeing with the child. What it does mean is that you listen to your players, understanding and empathizing with what they are feeling at the moment. Remember, if a youngster is telling you something, it is real, it is important. Being an understanding adult shows that we recognize and care about how our athletes feel. You will be in a much better position to offer guidance if the child feels that you understand.

Respect

We all want respect. Kids are no different. The problem is that we as adults tend to think we know the answers and hand out our own agendas. We tell the kids the right way to do something, often in an effort to save time. Children do not respect adults who do this; they are not being taught to think independently.

Kids like the opportunity to voice their opinions. Our children enjoy the feeling of being respected that accompanies being asked by an adult their thoughts on a subject.

One way to create this kind of learning environment is to begin conversations as if the child is an adult. Use the same tone, emphasis, and respect that you would with a colleague. Most children will rise to the level of our expectations. When the child begins to act like a child, then we have to treat him as a child. This is a great teachable moment. Explain to the child that you treated him as if he were an adult and explain where he fell short of your expectations. Players will respect you for acting positively and constructively, not deriding or making fun of them.

Direction

Guidelines, boundaries, limits, rules, consequences—these are terms from the structure of games. They are the parameters. It is important for the adult to reinforce this structure, to offer direction to the children. Just as a Little League field needs foul lines and rules, kids need behavioral guidelines. If, for example, having a clean bench and sidelines is an important team goal, you need to state this rule and the consequences of leaving equipment lying around. Children need to know what the guidelines and boundaries are. If you have created a strong relationship with your team, they will be receptive to your direction. That is why it is important to do this from the beginning and to be consistent. (Chapter Eight discusses rules and consequences.)

Limits

This is related to direction. Children need limits in order to understand what is appropriate and what is not. Just as the umpire uses the foul line to indicate what is fair and what is foul, you need to set limits on behavior. Children need to know that they will not be allowed to put down other players and officials; they also need to know the consequences of such behavior. Someone once said that "a lack of boundaries and consequences is a form of child abuse." That might sound a bit harsh, but it makes the point.

Independence and Responsibility

So far there has been a lot of talk about spending time and developing relationships with the children on your team. There are also times when children need to be separate and independent. An effective coach knows when an athlete needs to be alone or be encouraged to develop a sense of independence. The ultimate goal is to provide the athletes with the confidence they need to develop on their own.

Building Team Spirit

Team unity and team spirit, important to all good teams, do not happen by chance. What promotes unity and spirit? One way is for the team to come together to share activities other than sports. Shared experiences, whether formal activities such as team meetings or informal gatherings such as trips, barbecues, or challenge games, will build relationships. These times are especially important for younger children to show them how close the team is.

It is also helpful for children to see adults in positions other than authority roles. Informal experiences help children see the coach as a person with interests, feelings, and roles outside coaching.

Although the feeling of being part of a team is very important to children, experiences that create this spirit of unity are often overlooked. The reasons are simple: Get-togethers, trips, and other group activities take time and are not often viewed by adults as necessary aspects of the season. Adults are used to the essentials—practice and play. To the kids, however, these extra experiences are significant. You might feel that there is not enough time for such get-togethers. But if you invest time early in the season in getting to know your athletes, creating shared experiences, the time spent will pay off through better understanding and more respect. The cohesion developed will result in better teamwork and probably more success on the field.

Coach's Tip—get some parents involved with planning these extras. Check out your town's high school athletic schedule and attend one of their games or a local college game. Have the kids challenge the parents in a game.

Summary

Children learn as much from how we act than from what we say. As a coach, you must remain aware of the tremendous influence you have over the children on your team. It is vital to remember that your behavior and actions are watched by them. They are learning simply by watching how you behave.

Positive and healthy relationships form the foundation for a team that respects and values all its members. Enforcing rules and dealing with difficult issues will be easier and more productive for teams that have spent the time developing healthy relationships. The resulting message of caring will ensure that your players are listening and learning positive life lessons.

CHAPTER SEVEN

Learning Through Dialogue

Coach Win-at-All-Costs never listens to what his players say, nor does he encourage them to discuss what might be on their minds. Noah tells his friend Josh, who plays on Coach Goodsport's team, that they never discuss anything. Coach Win-at-All-Costs does all the talking—usually by yelling. Both Noah and Josh are realizing that there are a lot of differences between the two teams.

Josh feels comfortable on Coach Goodsport's team because they do talk about what goes on during the games. Josh feels that it is easier to understand the whole idea of teamwork when the coach and team spend time discussing how the players can put it into practice. Coach Win-at-All-Costs only yells, "Let's work as a team!" and does that only if he thinks it will help win the game. Coach Goodsport gathers the team before and after the game and really listens to what the children have to say. She asks them questions that make them think.

Josh's parents notice the difference too. They are especially happy about the amount of time Coach Goodsport spends talking with her team. Josh's parents believe that this interactive exchange is a good way for the children to learn.

❖

Teachers have long known the value of round table or interactive dialogue in the learning process. Recent research shows that children whose families engage in dinnertime conversations do better in school. Children today need opportunities to talk with significant adults more than at any other period in history. On average, adults spend less than seven minutes a day talking with their children. Sports provide many opportunities for dialogue about important issues. As a coach and role model, you are in an excellent position to take advantage of these learning opportunities.

The Value of Interactive Dialogue

Children, like adults, learn through discussing important issues with others who listen and provide constructive feedback. Dialogue is an important part of the learning process because the continuous back-and-forth exchange challenges people's minds. In a sense, interactive dialogue challenges the mind similarly to the way sports exercise and challenge the body. Take, for example, how Coach Goodsport has learned to incorporate the dialogue process to teach the concept of perseverance.

Coach Goodsport realizes that she cannot simply yell, "You need to be persistent!" The children may hear the command but will not understand what to actually do. Coach Goodsport learned early in her coaching career about the value of engaging children in interactive dialogue, challenging them to think through and discuss questions and ideas.

Coach Goodsport offers a goal, in this case perseverance, and then creatively crafts a series of questions to help the children understand what perseverance actually looks like and what specific behaviors support it.

"What do you think perseverance means?" she asks them at a Warm-Up session before practice.

Usually the players' remarks are pretty general, such as "Perseverance means playing harder," "Not giving up," or "Not quitting when you strike out."

Coach Goodsport takes this learning opportunity further by asking players to think a little harder. "What does perseverance look like?" The children's responses begin to focus on perseverance-like behaviors, such as "staying positive" or "cheering on a teammate after striking out with the bases loaded." "If we stay positive even when we are down, we are helping the team." Coach Goodsport now sees the opportunity to reward these slightly more advanced notions of perseverance with praise. At the same time, she stretches her team's thinking further by asking them what they can all do to encourage and practice perseverance.

The point is that, while children learn through observing others, they also learn by having opportunities to think about and discuss issues with others. In the above example, Coach Goodsport could have just told the players what to do and they might have done it. But this would not have challenged their thinking nor exercised their minds. The back-and-forth exchange of ideas, questioning, reflection, acting, feedback, and goal setting are all part of the dialogue process.

Mutual Dialogue Versus the Coach's Pep Talk

Mutual dialogue suggests that there is a balance of input from each participant. One player makes a point and other players ask questions and offer their perspectives. The traditional coach's pep talk is not mutual dialogue, it is a lecture. It does not stimulate critical thinking in the same way that interactive dialogue does.

Unfortunately, some of us think that mutual dialogue means relinquishing control. The fact is that the opposite is true. The adult who is a strong leader knows how to use an interactive discussion to empower the players. It improves their understanding and sense of ownership of the process.

The coach's role is to ask the right questions to frame and steer the discussion. This helps the children begin to work out their own answers. Give children directions or answers and they will go along with very little thinking on their part. Asking them how *they* think the batting order should be organized or what should be done about a disrespectful act requires the children to think things through both from an individual and team point of view.

How to Promote Dialogue

In the previous chapter we looked at being a positive role model, creating an atmosphere of respect, and fostering good relationships. If you create a positive atmosphere, the task of engaging the children in dialogue will not be difficult. There are a number of other ingredients that can make your task easier and help ensure that the dialogue taking place is constructive, presenting real opportunities to learn.

Be a Facilitator, Not a Lecturer

Getting the kids talking is not the hard part. The more difficult task will be keeping the kids focused, not letting the discussion go too far astray, or get into critiques of individual performances. Your role here is one of facilitator rather than lecturer. Let the kids direct the discussion, with you giving a nudge here and there to keep them on track.

Ask the Right Questions

One way to promote dialogue is to ask the players for their understanding of the skills you have introduced. When introducing responsibility, for example, Coach Goodsport asks her players to define responsibility. She then uses their remarks to ask them about other examples of responsibility. The continuous dialogue between the players and the coach requires the entire team to engage in critical thinking. This process stimulates their understanding of both team and individual goals and advances their understanding of the concept being taught. This deeper understanding of responsibility helps children begin to see how it can be seen and practiced away from the sports experience.

Stretch the Players' Thinking

When Coach Goodsport first asked her team what they thought responsibility meant, the responses were relatively general. At each team meeting, she presents new questions to stretch the children's thinking. For example, once the children understand that "bringing your equipment to practice" is one responsibility of being a participant on a team, Coach Goodsport then challenges the children to move to a higher level of understanding of what other responsibilities they might have both on and off the playing field.

Allow Time for Reflection

The process of dialogue is an ongoing activity that includes a number of phases. Once Coach Goodsport has set teamwork as a goal and challenged the players to reach a higher level of understanding, she needs to allow the players some time to reflect on what they have learned and what is now being asked. Close a Warm-Up or Cool-Down meeting with a summary of the discussion and leave your players with a question that challenges them to stretch their understanding even further. You might ask, for example, that each player come to the next practice with two examples of what teamwork looks like at home or in their classroom. This period of personal reflection allows for clarification and sets the stage for further dialogue.

Feedback on Goals

Once a goal has been defined and the players challenged to understand higher levels of behavior, the coach needs to offer feedback on their progress. The feedback begins the dialogue process again, but you will be at a higher level of understanding than you were before.

How and Where to Incorporate Dialogue

The first reaction of many coaches when asked to spend time talking with their players is "When? I don't have enough time now!" While the Warm-Up and Cool-Down sessions are designed to incorporate interactive dialogue into the youth sports experience, the process of dialogue can be used in many situations and for many reasons. Use the basics of interactive dialogue anytime you are addressing issues with the children or with an individual child. *And it will eventually save you time.* Mutual dialogue not only helps to teach children basic values, but it provides a window into the children's hearts and minds.

Summary

Dialogue is an interactive process between the coach and players and among the players themselves. It includes asking questions, listening, responding, thinking, reflecting, and offering feedback. Dialogue is a process that respects all the participants and values what each person has to say. It provides the coach with opportunities to be a teacher, and a setting in which to ask questions and challenge the children to stretch themselves intellectually.

Interactive dialogue strengthens the learning process. People learn by being exposed to opportunities to express their ideas and share their feelings within a respectful environment. The healthy exchange of ideas within a supportive setting challenges children to think critically, reflect, and put their new learnings into action.

Too often we move so fast, not really understanding how our players think and feel. If you take the few moments necessary to understand your young athletes, you will be in a much better position to motivate the children and challenge them with new levels of expectations. Dialogue, used effectively and as part of the PLUS model, helps to create a positive team climate that increases the likelihood that a team will play harder and in a more focused way. A team whose players understand, respect, and listen to each other plays better together.

CHAPTER EIGHT

Learning Through Rewards and Consequences

Early in the season, Coach Neophyte told the players on his third-grade basketball team that they had to come to practice if they wanted equal playing time in the games. He also said that he liked players who had good attitudes and were team players. Gordon Goodsport likes Coach Neophyte because he is young and cool. Gordon is not a great athlete, but he followed what Coach Neophyte said about coming to practice, working hard, and having a positive attitude.

On the other hand, Slam-Dunk Sam is a good basketball player who doesn't have the greatest attitude. He sometimes swears and trash talks to other players. He misses practices when he feels like it. In the championship game at the end of the season, Gordon was surprised and disappointed that he did not get to play while Sam played most of the game. Afterwards, Gordon told Coach Neophyte that he didn't think he would play basketball next year. Gordon followed the rules Coach Neophyte set but was not rewarded for his behavior. Sam was rewarded for his behavior in not following the rules. Gordon is confused.

❖

Everyone is learning something from this experience. Gordon is learning that rules are bent in the interest of winning. Sam is learning that he does not have to follow the rules set for the rest of the team because he is such a naturally skilled player. Coach Neophyte is realizing that he has a pretty big influence on his players. He wasn't thinking about what Gordon or the team thought or felt, he was thinking about putting the most talented players on the court. He was thinking only about winning.

As coaches, we need to be aware of the ways that we reward children. How you respond to questions, how you respond to a child's skills, how you respond to behavior will be viewed by children in a positive or negative way. Do you spend more time coaching the better-skilled or more motivated players? Do you kid around with or talk more with these players? Do you reserve the best positions and playing time for your team favorites?

Children associate behavior with the response it gets. This may sound simplistic, but the point to keep in mind is that we are often not aware of what values and behaviors we are rewarding or punishing. If, for example, your team has a rule that says you must come to practice in order to receive equal playing time, but you then overlook the rule when your best player misses practice for no reason, think about just what you are rewarding. The children will figure this out and see that they are rewarded for being skilled, not necessarily for following team rules and team values.

Creating an Environment that Rewards the Right Values

Developing the physical structure of the PLUS cycle provides the environment in which learning can occur. Associating specific behaviors with the PLUS core values helps your players begin to recognize examples of the values as they happen. To be certain that the right behaviors are reinforced, you need a system that incorporates the third way in which children learn: through rewards and consequences.

Connecting Rules to Values

Because children usually know what they need in order to have a respectful and safe environment, they should be actively involved in designing their team's rewards and consequences system. Take Gordon Goodsport's example. Gordon believed in the value of being on time and developing a respectful and positive attitude. He also agreed that being late, skipping practices, and developing a negative attitude are not good. Coach Neophyte could have talked with his team before the season and asked the kids to decide what the consequences would be when someone skipped practice or displayed a negative attitude. Children will often be tougher than adults.

In Gordon's case, at least two ingredients of a respectful team environment are missing. The first is that Coach Neophyte did not follow his own rules. Neither did he involve the players in making the rules in the first place and setting possible consequences for breaking them.

The second missing element is a process for the team to come together and engage in productive, interactive dialogue. Coach Neophyte and his team have not developed a structure or environment where all the team members can discuss the rules and how to deal with infractions.

*"Your actions are so loud
I can't hear what you are saying!"*

Connect Actions to Words

Another mistake Coach Neophyte made is that he did not make a clear connection between what he values (being on time and a positive attitude) and rewards (playing time). Children need clear and consistent guidelines and connections. The following diagram illustrates how values, rules, and consequences are related.

Value	Rule	Reward/Consequence
Respect	No put-downs	Apology
Perseverance	Play your best	First choice of position
Responsibility	Be on time for games	Sit out first portion of game
Fair Play	Share positions	Recognition
Teamwork	Work together	Choice of position, recognition

Using the above format, you can pick a value like respect, make rules that support that value—"no put downs"—and agree on a consequence for being disrespectful—a public apology or sitting out a portion of a game.

When related back to your team's values, all rules and interactions must have unified meaning. Each value, each rule, each part of the system can be observed and understood through specific actions. Making Warm-Up and Cool-Down sessions a regular part of the team environment allows time for sorting out difficult and confusing issues. By using this process, you will provide opportunities to encourage moral and intellectual development by making the most of teachable moments.

Creating Team Rules

Developing rules that support your philosophy and core values involves the following steps:

1. **Formulate Rules**—that support the values of the team. Use Warm-Up and Cool-Down sessions early in the season to discuss what each value means, in behavioral terms, and then develop specific rewards and consequences. Continue revisiting this process as the season progresses. Add new rules if behaviors occur that detract from team values.

2. **Create a Rules Poster**—Players can have fun making their own rules poster. Better yet, a soccer ball or baseball bat to write the rules on creates a sort of team icon or mascot. The team can assign a player to bring the bat or ball to games and practices as a reminder of the team's rules.

3. **Create Systems for Recognition**—that allow ample opportunity for players to be recognized as important members of the team when players actively model the team's values. Remember to catch children doing something right more often than doing something wrong. This can be done on both a formal and an informal basis.

4. **Create Reward and Disciplinary Actions**—that are specific to supporting rules and that reflect team values; i.e., what happens when there is a put-down?

5. **Develop a Process**—where all players are responsible for monitoring rule infractions. Set up a system for reporting infractions that does not cause a player to feel embarrassed or picked on.

6. **Use Interactive Dialogue**—to discuss rules, rule infractions, and how rules support team values. Use dialogue as a medium for helping the players understand why a team has rules and the connections between team values and the rules supporting them.

Ingredients for Developing Team Rules

Just as there are ingredients for being a positive role model and for using dialogue to promote positive learning, there are several things you can do to make the creation of rewards and consequences go smoothly.

- Always focus on the underlying value, not just on the rule. Stress why the value is important and why behavior that models the value contributes positively to the team environment.

- Be creative in developing rewards and consequences. Involve the players and have some fun, especially when deciding on consequences. (The punishment should fit the crime.)

- Remember the two other ways we've discussed in which children learn. Coach Neophyte got into trouble because he did not model his own rules, nor did he use dialogue to discuss issues with the children.

Using Goals

One way to make sure that you create a reward system that supports your team values is to understand everyone's goals, including your own, your players', and the parents'. Most parents want their children to gain confidence and learn sportsmanship, teamwork, and an understanding of fair play by playing sports. If these values are to be encouraged, they need to be shared and communicated as common team goals.

Not all children are excellent athletes, and their self-esteem may suffer as a result of an over emphasis on natural ability and technical skills. Coaches and parents often reserve praise and rewards for the better athletes. Rewarding children for actively supporting your team values, not just for scoring the most points, ensures that all your players will learn important lessons.

■ *What happens when:*

A player puts down a teammate?

Players harass or trash talk the other team?

A player kicks another player's soccer ball or throws a teammate's glove at practice?

One way to help get the parents to support your program more actively is by telling them your team values and goals and asking them to think about their own goals. This helps ensure that, as you develop a system of rewards and consequences, you will have their understanding and support.

The Players' Goals

Involving your players in creating rules of behavior is one step toward developing a consistent system of rewards and consequences. Having players set goals for themselves is the next step, giving the children an active sense of involvement in the process. Goals have the advantage of ranging from skill development, like learning to be a better passer in soccer, to supporting team values, like learning the meaning of fair play by helping an opposing player up after a hard hit.

When setting goals, use the PLUS core values and the leader-to-detractor scale detailed in Chapter Four. Using the common language that defines the levels of the scale helps players understand where their behavior falls and allows them to think of behaviors that will move them up the scale.

Proper goal setting should help children set realistic challenges and monitor their progress. Goal attainment can be a very positive experience for young children; with proper guidance, goal setting can increase the likelihood of a positive and productive sports experience. It is important that coaches help the children define what their goals are and what they look like in behavioral terms. Coaches should describe different types of goals and teach children how to set individual goals that will improve performance, attitude, and effort.

To be most effective, goals should:

- Be understandable, measurable, and reachable (an end in sight). Long-term goals should be supported by attainable short-term goals.

- Involve children's input.

- Match children's interests, motivations, and talents.

- Be put in writing by the child.

- Be challenging yet attainable.

- Include both effort and performance in evaluation.

The Coach's Goals

Coach Neophyte professes to believe in not pushing children. He believes in the importance of skill development because that is how he was coached as an athlete. However, when his nine-year-old daughter, Sarah, joins his basketball team, he finds himself with emotions that are difficult to control. At one game, each time the ball goes down the court and his daughter is not in the midst of the play, he yells, "Get aggressive!" He is beginning to understand that his image is linked to his daughter's performance. He wants her to be a winner. He wants a winner as a daughter. Sarah feels the pressure and is not having much fun. Coach Neophyte needs to begin an important process of examining what is important to him as a coach, parent, and role model. Otherwise, Sarah's sense of self and overall personal growth may be endangered.

Once you have thought about why you coach, what you want to teach your players, and recognize your position as a role model, the next step is to set your own goals. This is a parallel step to take along with helping the children set goals for themselves and for the team.

Coach's goals might include the following:

- To treat all players fairly.

- To give the children opportunities to share their feelings.

- To be a positive role model.

- To ensure that all the children, regardless of their abilities, feel good about themselves and feel part of the team.

Parents' Goals

Parents can play a critical role in determining the quality of their children's sports experience—for better or worse. Children whose parents are informed, involved, and supportive are in luck. Many other parents, for a number of reasons, unnecessarily add to their children's stress in playing sports. Maybe they think their child is better than she really is. Or maybe the parent is living out his or her own unfulfilled sports aspirations. Maybe they feel that one way to compete with the neighbors is to have a talented and successful athlete. One thing is certain, youth sports are a very public and social activity. The influence that parents can have during a game is enormous. One role of the coach is to help shape these influences in ways that advance your team, values, and goals.

Many parents are not sure how to act or think about their child playing on a sports team. The coach can assist parents' understanding by informing them of the team's philosophy, values, and rules. Misunderstandings, potential difficulties, and even confrontations with parents can be avoided and diffused through direct communication. An information letter and questionnaire can be sent home to parents that informs them of the Sports PLUS philosophy and gives them an opportunity to share their basic goals and beliefs (see Appendix I). When goals are clearly stated and shared, it is easier to get support from parents.

"If my players write me a letter ten years from now, what will they say they learned playing on my team?"

Summary

What you reward can be a powerful teaching and learning experience. What you *really* reward teaches your players what you really value. The old saying that "your actions are so loud I can't hear what you are saying" is valid, especially to young children. As a coach, you need to be aware of what you are rewarding. And you need to be certain that your rewards and consequences support your team's core values.

Rules and consequences alone, however, will not necessarily teach values. You need to model your values and provide the children with opportunities to discuss what the values mean. Rules, procedures, and consequences are connected to the team's philosophy and values. When appropriately related back to the team's values, your team rules take on real meaning.

The Foundation of Team Character

Have you ever asked yourself why you coach? Or what you most want the children on your team to take away from their experience? What if your players write a letter to you ten years from now. What will they say? What have you taught them?

One of the first steps all coaches need to take in order to answer these questions is to develop an individual and team philosophy to youth sports. How you prioritize winning, fun, personal development, and the importance of self-confidence rest on your philosophy and the values you and your team identify as the most important.

• CHAPTER NINE •

Developing a Team Philosophy

Noah loves baseball, but he hasn't had much success. He is a decent runner but has never been able to hit the ball. The league mandates that all the players play in every game, but that doesn't really help Noah. Coach Neophyte always finds ways to distribute the playing time and positions so that the better players are in the game when winning is at risk. On this particular Saturday, Coach Neophyte is in a position he hates—he is losing late in the game. It is the bottom of the seventh inning and Noah is due up. Noah has played enough innings to pass the league requirements, so Coach Neophyte could take him out of the game. But Noah wants to bat. And though most of the team wants Noah to bat, Tommy-Too-Cool and his buddies are making some not-so-subtle comments. They don't want Noah to bat because they want to win more than anything else.

On the other side of the field, a similar situation occurred the inning before. Josh, who is not the greatest pitcher, was due to pitch the sixth and seventh innings. Although the game was close, Coach Parent believes that it is important to distribute the playing time equally, and if a player wants a shot at pitching they have the right—even if their ability might put winning the game at risk. Coach Parent is very clear on how he prioritizes development, fun, and winning.

Noah wonders whether Coach Win-at-All-Costs is going to pull him for a better batter.

What would you do if you were Coach Neophyte? Why? Do you agree with Coach Parent? Why? Why not? What are the most important aspects of youth sports, and how do you deal with situations where your beliefs are tested?

How you attempt to answer these important questions—and others—stems from your philosophy regarding youth sports, how you prioritize and balance conflicting interests, and your most basic beliefs about children and competition.

Most volunteer coaches, who are usually parents of players, do not begin the season with a clear sense of what they value (I would guess that most parents have never developed a philosophy of youth sports). It is important to consider some basic questions about your personal philosophy and values. If you don't, you may send mixed messages to the children, messages that they will interpret as what you truly value, regardless of what you might say.

Developing Your Philosophy

Webster's dictionary defines philosophy as "the rational investigation of the truths and principles of being, knowledge, or conduct." OK, but what does that mean to me, as a coach or parent of children involved in youth sports? The dictionary goes on to define philosophy as "a system of principles for guidance in practical affairs." Better. The first step in forming your philosophy of youth sports is to examine the principles on which you want to build your sports program.

Without a strong foundation to guide the *practical affairs* of your team, the weaknesses will become apparent when you are called on to make difficult decisions. Once developed, your team's philosophy will guide such practical issues as equal playing time, the children's attitudes about winning and losing, and how your players treat one another. A team's philosophy also influences how a team establishes its rules and consequences and how issues of fairness and teamwork are treated. Developing a consistent, well-thought-out philosophy is one of the most important first activities of any good youth sports team.

The first step in developing your philosophy is to examine your own beliefs and values in the area of youth sports and to ask yourself some fundamental questions:

- Why do I coach?

- What are my goals as coach?

- What values do I want the children on my team to transfer beyond their sports experience into their daily lives?

- In what order of value do I rank winning, personal development, and having fun?

- What type of people do I want to develop?

- What is my most important role as coach?

The next step is to discuss with your players what their philosophy might be. To help them get started, ask them some basic questions:

- Why do you want to play on this team?

- What are the most important things about playing?

- What does teamwork mean to you?

- What are your goals as a player on this team?

- What does it mean to be a "good player"?

Involving your players will ensure that the children on your team feel a strong sense of ownership and pride in their team's philosophy and will follow it on their own, without constant prodding from you.

Before you do this, I would like to expand on the Sports PLUS philosophy introduced in Chapter Two. It is not my intention to set down my own system of principles and tell you that this is the way it must be done. Rather, I offer the PLUS philosophy as a guide, a place for you to begin when considering and developing your own values and the order in which you prioritize them.

The Sports PLUS Philosophy: Philosophy by Choice

The Sports PLUS philosophy grew out of my research at Harvard University and 20 years of working with well over 1,000 young athletes. It was developed to provide a template to "guide the practical affairs" of a youth sports program. These ten principles comprise the Sports PLUS philosophy and represent what I believe to be the most important values on which to build a strong team foundation. If you agree that the following principles make sense, the next step is to put them into action.

The Sports PLUS philosophy consists of ten basic beliefs that help coaches create a sports environment that emphasizes fun, personal development, and positive values.

1. *Sports should be structured to promote self-confidence.*

   The most important aspect of youth sports is how the experience makes the children feel. Above everything else—tournaments, uniforms, winning, who plays where and when—lies this fundamental principle that we must create an environment that builds confidence for all the children.

2. *Sports should encourage and develop positive character values.*

   Self-esteem without positive character is a one-sided coin. It is our responsibility, as coaches and parents, to organize the sports environment to promote values that we agree are important. The five fundamental core values can and should be taught through the youth sports experience.

3. *Playing time should be distributed evenly.*

   For children under 12, it is important to distribute playing time equally among all players. To do otherwise undermines our first principle: to promote confidence in *all* the players. Our goal is to provide equal access for all children to opportunities for growth.

4. *Positions should be distributed evenly.*

   Learning to see the game from different positions encourages respect and understanding of all positions on the team and promotes intellectual development.

5. ***Rules and consequences should be clearly spelled out and enforced fairly and consistently.***

   Team rules must support the team's values. Clearly specified rules of conduct that all players understand and adhere to ensure the development of personal responsibility and consistent behavior.

6. ***Coaches and parents must model the values they want their children to learn.***

   The behavior of parents and coaches will affect the overall development of young children more than any other factor. We must act in ways that show that we value the ideals we teach our children.

7. ***It is our responsibility to help all children realize their personal potential.***

   You need to understand where each child is in their own developmental process. As coaches, we must understand that each child is different and that children develop at different rates.

8. ***Respect and responsibility form the foundation and moral fabric of a community.***

   Through the sports experience we can expand our children's awareness of, respect for, and responsibility to themselves, their community, their teammates, and the world in which they live.

9. ***Teaching the whole child requires the involvement of the whole community.***

   All community stakeholders, including parents, teachers, neighbors, and coaches, need to take an active interest in the growth of our children. Within this whole-community approach, coaches of youth sports teams are in a unique and powerful position to present a positive learning environment.

10. ***Winning and losing are only the end result of a game.***

    The actions and language of coaches and parents must reflect that winning and losing are only one part of the whole process of any youth sports experience. Winning should never be the ultimate goal of a youth sports team.

While you may disagree with some of the above principles or the order in which they are ranked, the important point is to get you thinking about these key issues when developing your own philosophy. How do *you* feel about these statements? Take a few moments to carefully consider each one and the order in which they are ranked.

Developing Your Own Team Philosophy

Before you consider the philosophy prioritization chart on page 103, I'd like to present some additional ingredients for you to keep in mind when thinking about and then prioritizing your team philosophy.

Becoming a Leader: Personal Versus Team Philosophy

We all have our own personal beliefs about sports and competition, most likely influenced to a great extent by our individual experiences with sports. But no matter what your personal sports experience, you take on a new responsibility when assuming a leadership position as the coach of a children's sports team. As coach, you accept the responsibility to create a sports experience that is fun, fair, and challenging for each player.

Because this can be a challenging task for many coaches, it is critical to take stock of your personal beliefs and ask yourself how your own personal sports experience influences your philosophy and how you run your team.

Conflicts and Priorities

We all want our children to have fun and develop as healthy, well-rounded people. That's a pretty easy philosophy to agree on. The difficulties arise when values and priorities come into conflict. Consider this situation: It is late in an important soccer match. Your team is down by one goal and your weakest goalie is due to go into the game. Your team philosophy states that all athletes should have opportunities to play the positions they want and this child has been practicing hard to be a goalie. What would you do? Why?

This is why prioritizing your values and articulating your team's philosophy are so crucial. It is also why informing the players' parents of the team philosophy and being able to explain it to them is critical. When conflicts like the above situation do arise, you can make the right, though not always easy, decision. Having a well-defined philosophy that players and parents understand provides consistency and a rationale for your decisions as coach and, as discussed in Chapter Six, makes you a positive role model for both the players and the parents.

The Pressure Question

Even in the best team environments, there may be times when a child feels a great deal of pressure, if only from their own perception of the situation. Is equal playing time then *always* right? What about the child? How does he feel? Maybe he doesn't want to pitch in the last inning or play goalie because he thinks that he might make the team lose.

The first answer is that if you have created an environment where players respect one another and the players feel supported by their teammates, then a player will not feel overly pressured. Still, there may be times when you need to consider the pressure felt by a child, whether real or perceived. Remember that number one in the PLUS philosophy is to build self-confidence. A pressure situation presents one of those points where priorities can conflict. You, as the child's coach, need to make decisions with the best interest of the child in mind.

No Matter What, Keep It Fun

Fun is the number one reason children participate in youth sports programs. Having fun is participating in meaningful activities, being with people who don't yell and who offer encouragement. Fun is using a ball, bat, glove, stick, or racquet as often as possible. It is hitting baseballs, shooting hoops, pitching balls, kicking goals, splashing water, playing games, being with friends, eating ice cream or pizza. Fun is not being yelled at. It is not being on a team that fights and argues. Fun is not enduring long boring practices, coaches who talk too much and don't listen, or sitting on the bench too long.

Fun is being understood, having a coach who cares about the team and who knows the game and how to execute the skills, having shared team experiences, learning new sports skills. Fun is not having a coach who does not understand what it is like to be a child, having a coach who doesn't know the game, having a team that has no spirit or unity, not learning the technical aspects of the game.

Creating a climate of fun for your team means that the children will practice and play harder, taking a personal interest in their team, in each other, and in their own learning. It can make a big difference in how the children play—as a team or simply as a group of individuals—if all your players truly enjoy the sports experience you create for them.

Have you ever watched a team where a few players dominate the play and get far more playing time than others? Where the athletes play as individuals rather than as teammates? Teams like this rarely provide a climate of fun for the children. Even if the team wins, many of the children will not feel truly part of the team. Eventually they will lose, and even the best players will be disappointed with the process. Many of them will not be having much fun. Remember, in order to keep the internal fires burning, you must keep it fun.

Encourage Good Athletes and Good People

This sounds simple, but this basic philosophy provides us with a benchmark for evaluating the sports experience. When confronted with dilemmas ask yourself: "Does this behavior encourage good athletes and good people? If not, what lesson *is* being taught?" Sports can help children develop both as athletes and as people. Life skills such as teamwork, respect, responsibility, and leadership are important for both sports and throughout life.

What Do the Children Think?

Considering your own philosophy towards youth sports is the first step in creating the philosophy for your team. The next step is to get the players involved. After all, this is their game. The best way to understand what the children think is to find out what is on their minds. This can be accomplished through Warm-Up and Cool-Down sessions. Spend a few sessions early in the season discussing what your philosophy is and then getting the children to offer their views and formulate their own philosophy. Revisit the team philosophy during the season as needed and refer to it when discussing issues and conflicts and to illustrate learning opportunities.

Prioritizing Your Philosophical Principles

After considering the above ingredients, ask yourself a few very basic questions:

Why do I think children play sports?

What is my role as the coach?

Should the better players play more? Why?

Is winning more important than children's development?

What other issues are important to me?

Once you have answered these questions, it is time to prioritize your team philosophy. Here, once again, are the ten items from the PLUS philosophy. Consider each one and the hierarchy in which they are presented. Then fill out the team philosophy form with your personal youth sports philosophy.

1. Sports should be structured to promote the self-confidence of all the players.

2. Sports should encourage and develop character values such as teamwork, respect, responsibility, fairness, and perseverance.

3. Playing time should be distributed evenly.

4. Positions should be distributed evenly.

5. Rules and consequences should be clearly spelled out and enforced fairly and consistently.

6. Coaches and parents must model the values they want their children to learn.

7. It is our responsibility to help all children realize their personal potential.

8. Respect and responsibility form the foundation and moral fabric of our community.

9. Teaching the whole child the requires the involvement of the whole community.

10. Winning and losing are only end results of a game.

Communicate Your Philosophy

Developing a team philosophy with your players is one step in the process. The next step should be to communicate your philosophy to the parents. This will help avoid conflicts. Probably the simplest way to be sure that all parents have an opportunity to see the team philosophy is to make copies and send them home with the children. This gives the parents the chance to discuss with their children how they developed the philosophy and what it means to them. You can also create a team philosophy chart. Post it at practices and games where it can be seen. Talk about it with parents whenever you have the opportunity.

Get creative and put your team philosophy on a soccer ball or a baseball bat. Get the children involved by letting them write the statements. Doing this will show that their philosophy is real and meaningful, something that they themselves created. Coaches can use this bat or ball when the team is acting in ways that go against the team philosophy. The coach can just roll out the ball and ask, "What is going wrong here? Can anyone share our philosophy with the team? What do we need to do?" This type of interaction puts the responsibility back on the players and gives them a chance to discuss what is important, what is going wrong, and what they need to do to get their behavior back on track.

Summary

Developing a positive and consistent philosophy is the first and most important step in assuring that our children have a positive sports experience. With a stated team philosophy that the coaches, the players, and their parents all understand, your decisions will be clear and consistent. While there will still be difficult decisions to make, with your philosophy as a guide you will be sure that your decisions are consistent with the team's stated beliefs.

The Philosophical
Principles of the: _____

1. _____
   _____

2. _____
   _____

3. _____
   _____

4. _____
   _____

5. _____
   _____

6. _____
   _____

7. _____
   _____

8. _____
   _____

9. _____
   _____

10. _____
    _____

Defining a Team's Core Values

After the players shake hands, Coach Goodsport gathers her team of soccer players around the bench for a Cool-Down meeting. They have just won their fifth straight game by a landslide, and a lot of players and coaches are saying they are the best team in the league. Of course, a lot of strong feelings typically arise when kids play organized sports and adults are involved. Some players are psyched because they are winning; children on other teams are bummed because they hate losing. Tommy-Too-Cool is bragging at school that he is on an undefeated team. On the other side of the field, Coach Win-at-All-Costs is yelling at his team for losing. He is certainly not showing respectful behavior to his players. Timid Teresa wants to play more and is thinking about quitting.

Even though her team won, Coach Goodsport is concerned about her team's attitude. A couple of players forgot that they were responsible for bringing the after-game treats. And toward the end of the game, once they got ahead, the children didn't seem to play as hard. They didn't show much teamwork in their victory, and a couple of players made cocky remarks as they went through the post-game congratulating line. One of Coach Win-at-All-Costs' players knocked down one of Coach Goodsport's players and the ref didn't see it. Coach Goodsport didn't say anything but knows it is time for a Cool-Down meeting and a discussion about the importance of fair play.

As the children form a circle, Coach Goodsport asks her team what they thought of the game. The responses were typical for nine-year-olds. "We are awesome!" "It was fun to win!" "Are we going to the tournament if we keep winning?" "We killed them!" "I think we ought to let Tommy play the whole game." Coach Goodsport realizes that she is in the midst of a teachable moment.

❖

Your team philosophy and values are related. Believing in equal playing time (a philosophical belief) is a form of fairness (a value). Your team's values grow out of its philosophy. The purpose of this chapter is to take your philosophy and put it into values that are observable and measurable in the behavior of coaches, players, and even parents. Giving concrete guidelines to such abstract notions as respect and responsibility helps children recognize an instance of disrespect when it unfolds during practice or in a game. This chapter will provide you with the tools to recognize and address your team's values in an educational way.

Defining and Determining Values

Going to the dictionary again for help, we see that one definition of the word value is *that which is desirable or worthy of esteem for its own sake;…quality having intrinsic worth*. The problem we immediately run up against is in deciding just who decides what is desirable or worthy of esteem. People obviously have differing values. In considering what values are most important to you as a coach or parent of a child on a youth sports team, the five PLUS values that we have used throughout the book can be considered *universal core values*, those that we can all agree have intrinsic worth:

- Teamwork
- Responsibility
- Respect
- Fair Play
- Perseverance

The purpose of defining values, and then matching them to observable behaviors, is so that the values we speak of are understood by the children and presented as opportunities for learning. Simply yelling that *we need to do more teamwork* means nothing. Providing common language, behavioral definitions, and benchmarks provides everyone with a concrete understanding.

Values can be grouped into four general categories:

- **Intellectual**—Generally considered to be academic in nature, such as the ability to think clearly and critically.
- **Social**—Core values such as teamwork, conflict resolution, and cooperation can be considered social values.
- **Moral**—Issues of fairness, justice, and sportsmanship can be described as moral values.
- **Psychological**—Confidence and self-esteem can be described as psychological values.

Intellectual

The ability to think clearly, objectively, and critically are important life skills, particularly as we head deeper into the information age. As we see with Coach Goodsport's baseball program, sports can provide opportunities to help children develop their ability to think critically. Coach Goodsport's baseball program consciously promotes intellectual values by challenging the players to put into action the skills they have been practicing.

As a way to promote critical-thinking skills among her 11–12-year-old players, Coach Goodsport creates opportunities for her players to actively solve problems. Coach Goodsport worked all week on how playing time, positions, and batting order are organized and distributed. Then at the

Wednesday night game she sat back and let the kids run the game. She carefully observed, ready to intervene if necessary, as her team thought through the challenge of negotiating among themselves who was going to play where and when.

In this sense, game day, similar to exam day in school, becomes an opportunity for the team to demonstrate their thinking and leadership skills. The players become responsible for organizing the equipment and distributing playing time, positions, and batting order.

Coaches have an opportunity to play an important role in the intellectual development of their players by providing them with situations that challenge their abilities. We must also look for and be prepared to address teachable moments when they present themselves. This does not mean, however, that we turn the kids loose. You must be especially observant, ready to intervene and offer guidance as the children struggle with particularly difficult issues.

How to promote intellectual challenges:

- Begin practices with a Warm-Up session that outlines the goals of the day. Encourage players to lead the discussions (see Chapter Three).

- Let the team be in charge of positions and playing time during a practice scrimmage. Challenge them to devise game strategies and plays.

- Provide opportunities for players to discuss which values are most important for the team to embrace and why.

- Encourage players to create the rules and consequences that support the team values; i.e., respect is a value. "No put-downs" is a behavioral example of a rule that supports the value of respect, and "sitting out one inning" is a consequence for being disrespectful.

In order for children to accept the intellectual challenges offered to them, you must first create an environment where all players feel safe to speak up and offer ideas. A climate that actively promotes respect and a sense of fairness will give players a safe place in which to explore their own intellectual development. The children must know that when they offer an idea it will be listened to with respect.

Note: As the coach, you need to monitor this process. Do some players emerge as leaders? Do some players take advantage of others? Do some players help others reach their goals? Do all the player have an opportunity to speak? Which players tend to "hog" the best positions? Also, you must continue to divide the group into teams. Do not let children at this age level choose their own sides.

Social

> Tommy-Too-Cool is a good soccer player. Everyone knows it, including Tommy. Everyone wants Tommy on their team. He is even popular in school because he is a good athlete. There is really only one problem—Tommy doesn't listen and seldom passes the ball.

Cooperation, teamwork, and the ability to resolve conflicts are personal skills used throughout a lifetime. Tommy may be good in the youth leagues and his raw skill will probably carry him through for a while. Someday, however, he will need to learn how to work with others on a team; someday, knowing how to get along with others and contribute to a team effort will be an important life skill.

The ability to work effectively with people of both similar and differing views and backgrounds is essential. As children grow, they become increasingly involved with different types of groups. Families, school, church, clubs, and sports teams are examples of communities with shared values and common goals. Being a contributing member of a group or community is an important lifelong activity.

How to promote social values:

- Break the team into positions and require players to negotiate playing time among themselves.

- Require that all players in a basketball game touch the ball before anyone shoots.

- Have them read the book *Teammates,* by P. Golenbock, and discuss Peewee Reese and Jackie Robinson's relationship. What made these two different players such great teammates?

- Assign players a homework task to define teamwork and give an example of how they "do teamwork."

- Use a Most Valuable Person (MVP) exercise.

- Ask players to discuss how someone else on the team felt about a game.

- Rotate players through all positions so they see a variety of perspectives.

Note: Although the coach is in the background allowing the players to negotiate among themselves, it is the coach's responsibility to make sure that no one gets hurt, left out, or made fun of. One way to do this is to have a team rule that states "everyone will play the same amount." Although these rules will help, they won't make the process totally safe. Someone will always feel left out or try to take advantage of the situation. In these cases, the coach can either intervene while the incident is occurring or wait to discuss it during the Cool-Down.

Moral

> Gordon is a good athlete but not a great athlete. He works very hard, follows the rules of the team, and is always willing to help the less-skilled and younger athletes. However, Gordon is upset about how Coach Neophyte runs his team. Coach Neophyte says that sportsmanship is important and following the rules and being respectful are more important than winning. But actions speak louder than words, especially when Coach Neophyte puts the new kid in the starting lineup after he swore at the umpire in the last game. Gordon is learning a lot about fairness and leadership and how society values winning. What moral lessons is he learning?

How people treat one another on a team, at school, or at home are examples of moral-reasoning skills. Issues of responsibility, fairness, caring, justice, truth, and sportsmanship are considered moral values that can be put into action through youth sports. Learning to tell the truth, even if it is difficult, is one of the most important life skills we can teach our children.

One powerful way that people learn moral reasoning is through example. In our behaviors, we as parents and coaches provide a moral mirror for our children. People also learn moral reasoning by being provided opportunities to discuss their feelings with others. A third way people learn moral values is through rewards. Youth sports programs provide many opportunities for children to learn moral reasoning skills in all three of these areas.

As the coach, you are in a position to model appropriate behaviors, to provide a forum for the children to discuss moral issues, and to influence how attitudes and behaviors are rewarded. What moral values do you model? What moral values do you discuss with your team? What moral values do you reward?

How to promote moral values:

- Moral values and lessons are learned within caring communities. Teams can be caring communities when coaches, parents, and players model respect and responsibility in their dealings with others.

- The first step in teaching moral values is determining which values are important. Refer back to Chapter Two and the PLUS core values and add your own.

- Once your values have been determined, they should then be defined in behavioral terms so the children can understand exactly what a word like "respect" means.

- Children learn values by being given opportunities to think, feel, and act. A team that encourages players through thinking, feeling, and acting will have a good chance of promoting moral values.

- Employ interactive dialogue whenever possible. Interactive dialogue is different from the typical coach's talk. It is a give-and-take of ideas and feelings that promotes the intellectual and moral growth of everyone involved. Dialogue can be used best in Warm-Up and Cool-Down sessions.

Psychological

Timid Teresa loves to play sports and be with her friends. She used to love to play soccer when she was younger, because she got to play a lot and felt like she added something to the team. This fall, however, Teresa isn't enjoying soccer as much. She knows she is not as talented as her friends. She sits on the bench more than she did last year. She is thinking of quitting the team to follow other interests.

We all want our children to be confident and feel good about themselves. Self-esteem grows out of confidence and confidence grows out of meaningful experiences and continued success. In fact, how children feel about themselves is the single best predictor of success. Teams that function within a positive environment provide all players, no matter what their skill levels, with the same opportunities for building self-confidence. The Sports PLUS model helps deal with the *I'm always the last one to be picked* problem.

I also believe that it is important for our children to develop a healthy, positive sense of competition. Being able to compete with others and strive to be the best you can be is a lifelong activity. If they are to realize their goals, people need to have a healthy competitive spirit. Children need the motivation to achieve if they are to realize their potential as athletes and people. Motivation to achieve, confidence, self-esteem, and a positive sense of competitiveness are psychological goals that can be learned through playing organized youth sports.

How to promote psychological values:

- Emphasize and model internal versus external rewards. Internal rewards are those that come from knowing that you gave your best or are improving your skills. External rewards come from outside ourselves—winning, championships, and trophies. While these are all part of the game, it is a matter of emphasis. If children are not first motivated internally, they may lose interest if the external rewards are no longer there.

- Praise players for improvements and effort. Use mistakes to teach the correct way to do something, pointing out how practice will lead to future success.

- Always model a positive attitude, even when things aren't going well. Teach by example that losing a game shows which skills the team needs to work harder on.

- Praise individual players for incremental steps. It can mean a lot to a young soccer player to receive a pat on the back for making a good pass or clearing the ball well.

- Maximize personal meaning. Look for activities and stories that the players can personalize.

Defining your team's philosophy and values is the first step toward creating a positive learning environment. But it's only the first step. Unless you put your principles into everyday practice, it has simply been an interesting intellectual exercise. Refer back to Chapter Two and the PLUS leader-to-detractor scale for guidelines on creating a common language and a system for associating behaviors with values.

A Brief Note on Setting Realistic and Measurable Goals

Helping children set realistic goals is a valuable endeavor. Goal setting is important because it gives the child something specific to strive for. Goals should be attainable to build confidence, and measurable so that progress can be tracked.

You can and should address both individual and team goals. For example, a team goal might be "no put-downs!" A put-down can be easily observed and dealt with, pointing out to the child where he currently is on the leader-to-detractor scale. You can then set a goal for the child on how to move up the scale to a higher level. Infractions can also be discussed with the team, but be sure not to let a discussion single out any individual child for criticism. You can do this by treating any infraction as a team problem and then dealing with the child in private.

Discuss with each child individual goals that are meaningful to the child, measurable, and challenging yet reachable. For example, you have a good player who scores a lot of goals but rarely passes the ball, even when a teammate is open and in position. Discuss this with the child, pointing to the values of teamwork and fairness. Set specific goals that can be measured in short periods of time, like a practice scrimmage or a game. "Your goal is to make four good passes when you see an open teammate." You can later discuss with the child how she feels she did and clearly see whether she made the four passes.

Summary

A strong community is one that lives by the values it sets forth as its guiding principles, embraced by *all* its members. Defining your values in concrete behavioral terms ensures that the children will begin to relate notions like responsibility and fair play to situations beyond the playing fields. Using the scales from Chapter Four to measure behaviors gives us, as parents and coaches, the ability to recognize and take advantage of teachable moments. When a team transfers their values into a workable, tangible format, those values become living pieces of the youth sports experience, a part of the team culture that is understandable to children, parents, and coaches.

The Fourth Quarter

The PLUS Developmental Levels

Remember the number one reason children play sports? To have fun. And this holds as true for twelve-year-olds as it does for six-year-olds. The problem is that what might be fun to a six-year-old may no longer be fun to a twelve-year-old. Because what you emphasize and prioritize change depending on the age level of the children on your team, it is important to understand their developmental needs, abilities, and constraints.

These levels reflect an increasing understanding of the complexities of a team, sports related issues, and the role that the coach plays in the learning process. Organizing youth sports into levels helps us understand the age groups we are working with. But it is also vital to remain sensitive to the fact that all children are different. To attempt to describe children solely in terms of levels would not be wise.

CHAPTER ELEVEN

Level I
Under Eight

Coach Parent decided to coach his seven-year-old son Noah's Little League baseball team because he thought it would be fun. Coach Parent did not play much baseball as a kid but is happy to be part of Noah's first sports experience. He really does not know what to expect as he and Noah arrive for their first practice. As the players climb out of their parents' cars, Coach Parent wonders what the young athletes are thinking. He wonders why they want to play baseball in the first place. Are they nervous or scared? What about?

Coach Parent catches himself daydreaming and asks the team to get into a circle for a Warm-Up.

"How is everyone? Good! Does everybody know each other?"

"Yeah!" yell most of the players.

"Well then, Jenny, do you know who is sitting next to you?" asks Coach Parent.

"I don't know," she replied.

"It is important that we all know each other on our team. Does anyone know why?"

"Yeah, because they are on our team."

"Good, Rose. I am going to give everyone a number. After you get your number, we are going to break into two groups. I want each of the groups to get in a circle with a ball. I want the first person to pass the ball to the next person and say their own name and ask the other teammate their name. We will go around the circle in each group until everyone knows each other and then we will mix up the groups."

Coach Parent soon learns that even with the best intentions calm can quickly turn to chaos. The players began tossing the ball across the circle to players who they already know. Some forget the instructions and begin drifting off to other activities, such as picking clovers. Coach Parent realizes he needs some help in organizing his practice so it will be both fun and productive.

❖

Overly structured competitive games for children under seven are risky business. Some children begin highly competitive games at a young age and enjoy the lifelong benefits of their early sports experiences. Just as often, if not more so, highly competitive and pressured early sports experiences are cited as reasons for children's early exit from sports. There are a number of reasons why some children have positive sports experiences and others have negative ones.

What do the kids say? Remember, the number one reason kids say they play sports is to have fun. Conversely, the number one reason why they quit is because they are *not* having fun. One of the reasons that young children do not have fun is that the adults coaching and organizing the sports do not understand what is important to their young players, emphasizing the wrong things.

Little kids play on little fields. It would not make much sense to pitch to six-year-olds from major-league distances or to use a full-size soccer field for second graders. Smaller and lighter bats allow smaller children to swing at the ball with a motion that is appropriate to their stage of physical development. Smaller soccer balls and goals match their size and ability. As children grow in size and physical strength, their equipment and playing fields can also get larger.

This developmental difference occurs in the psychological and social domains as well. The goals, rules, relationships, and discussions need to be appropriate to the children's developmental stages if fun and personal growth are important goals. Activities that are not challenging enough will be boring; too competitive an environment may result in fear, insecurity, and eventually dropping out. Finding an appropriate balance is the key.

Learning to Cooperate

Team sports require the ability to take the perspective of others and subvert individual desires for the greater good of the team. But at this level of development children tend to think from one perspective, their own. They are unable to understand their coach's and teammates' points of view. Team sports also require a sustained level of attention, something that children at this developmental stage can do only for brief periods. This one-way thinking, coupled with their short attention spans, makes it very difficult for children at this age to understand a concept like "spreading out the field."

To learn the concepts of teamwork and team goals, young children need activities that not only encourage but *require* cooperation. Most of the goals of organized youth sports are competitive by nature and need to be restructured for children under eight. The rules of traditional sports such as soccer and basketball can be altered not only to deemphasize winning, but to *require cooperation* in order to reach individual and group goals. Simple rule changes, such as requiring that all forwards touch the ball before somebody shoots, force the players to think first about others and to coordinate their efforts. This kind of rule change influences their behavior and, just like any other sports skill, becomes a practiced part of how they play the game. Using dialogue during Warm-Up or Cool-Down sessions to connect how these actions relate to teamwork ensures that positive learning occurs.

Using Cooperative Games

In cooperative games, players work together to move the team toward a stated goal. Organizing games that *require* cooperation is more powerful in shaping behavior than coaches and parents yelling, "Let's play together!"

Individual players can advance their positions only by helping another player or players reach theirs. Emphasizing group cooperation, these modified games provide the foundation for children to move on to a more complex under-standing of teamwork. Appendix II provides a number of good games and activities that help young children learn to work together.

Ingredients for Working with Children Under Eight

Using the basic principles of the PLUS model, especially the Warm-Up and Cool-Down sessions, will go a long way toward creating an environment in which you can begin teaching sports skills to young children. As with many other pieces of the PLUS model, there are a number of ingredients to use when coaching children under eight.

> Before the start of practice, Coach Parent gathers his six- and seven-year-olds and begins the Warm-Up session with a discussion about safety rules. Coach Parent breaks the rules into categories. The first are rules that promote a physically safe place to play, such as not leaving equipment strewn around for others to trip over. He introduces stations where the players can practice their throwing and batting.
>
> Other rules, such as the rule that players can only praise their teammates—no put-downs!—ensure that the playing field is an emotionally safe place. Coach Parent also understands that the equal distribution of playing time and positions helps create a morally safe community. Coach Parent begins the session by asking his players if they have any rules they want to make. Most of the players say they want the coach to be nice and not to yell. Coach Parent agrees.

- **Create Rules That Promote Safety**

   Children's safety is always the first and foremost concern. Our number-one priority is to help all children feel safe physically and emotionally. If you involve the children in making safety rules and guidelines, they'll soon begin to understand the reasons for having them.

- **Fun**

   Children learn more when they are having fun. Remember what they say when we ask them why they play sports. So what is fun for six- and seven-year-olds? You need to be creative in making practice fun and exciting. Break up skill drills with some cooperative activities.

- **Participation**

  Children like to play as much as possible. Above all, keep the children involved. Design practices so that as many players as possible are involved in the action at all times. And remember the saying—*Let the Game Instruct*. Oftentimes, playing the game is what the kids want to do most. It is also where they learn the most. The following general tips may be helpful in increasing participation:

  All players play equal time.

  Don't keep score.

  Switch players on teams.

  Rotate positions.

  Require that no player can shoot twice consecutively.

  Require that all players touch the ball before shooting.

  Don't use goals.

  Require that the score stay even (if you keep score).

  Equate winning the game with best dribbling or best passing rather than number of goals.

  Keep the game ongoing from week to week as team members switch teams...no one ever loses.

  Talk about fun and development, not the score of the game.

  Create zones on the field or court with cones or rope and require players to play in separate zones.

  Rotate the players through different zones.

  Create new responsibilities and roles, such as scorer, equipment manager, referee, etc.

  Use small groups in skill practices.

Remember, kids at this level have short attention spans and are egocentric. Changing activities, roles, and positions often helps to keep their attention longer.

- **Provide Opportunities for Achievement and Success**

Young children need opportunities to succeed at their individual levels of development. Highly organized sports, where the emphasis is only on playing time and winning, focus on the more aggressive players and are dangerous for young children. Instead, games and activities should be structured to assure that all the players can enjoy success.

To the child who always hits the ball but has never hit a home run, a home run might be a success. On the other hand, to a youngster who has never hit the ball, a grounder or hard pop fly might mean success. It is important to recognize the individual aspirations of each child, their potential for success, and then help each player set goals that are both challenging and attainable. Players can then achieve incremental success at their own pace.

- **Encourage Life Skills**

Life skills such as listening while other players are talking can be learned early and last a lifetime. At this young age there will be many valuable teachable moments to address. Common incidents to address at this age include:

  name-calling

  fighting

  hogging the ball

  bunching around the ball

  shoving

  children wanting to sit out because they are mad, sad, or upset

Most of these are natural byproducts of young children playing competitve activities. The key is not to let them go unaddressed. All of these examples relate to other areas of the child's life,

including school and family relationships. The coach's role is to talk with the players about their behaviors and relate them to other areas of their lives they can understand. It sometimes makes sense to stop play and discuss what is going on. Because of their egocentric perspective and short attention spans, a quick break might be just what they need. When you resume play it can be helpful to change the activity and players to defuse previous conflicts.

- **Quiet the Chaos**

  Quite possibly the most difficult and frustrating experience adults encounter when coaching six- and seven-year-olds is organizing the chaos. Noise levels and lack of attention are common problems. Use the tips for structuring your Warm-Up session to help you create your sports classroom atmosphere. The children will quickly learn that this signals the time to focus on the coming game or practice. The sooner you begin to use these techniques to quiet the chaos, the less often you will have to shout to get their attention.

Summary

Understanding the capabilities of young children is critical in designing any successful youth sports program. Creating an atmosphere in which all children feel safe both emotionally and physically should be a goal for all coaches, but is especially important when coaching children under eight. This is their first experience playing organized sports. Overemphasis on winning, competition, and skills may lead to early dropouts.

Cooperative games have special value for children at this age. They are a bridge between the solitary play of younger children and the competitive play of older children. If structured to include cooperative components, competitive sports can prepare six- and seven-year-olds to participate at the next level, which tends to be more intense and competitive and presents the players with new and more complex challenges. More importantly, the lessons learned about cooperation, helping, and being a team member will have value throughout one's life.

• CHAPTER TWELVE •

Level II
Eight to Ten

Coach Goodsport understands what her eight-to-ten-year-old soccer players need to work on to achieve certain goals. To encourage teamwork, she modifies the rules of her scrimmages to require that all players touch the ball before a shot can be made. Tommy, a skilled player who tends to control the game, is required to think about who hasn't played the ball. At first, the players complain, but they soon realize that they are becoming better players and a better team.

Coach Goodsport also requires that no player make two consecutive goals.

All players must have a chance to score before the player who scored previously can attempt another shot. Similar changes can be made in basketball, baseball, hockey, and other youth sports. These adjustments *require* that all players contribute to the team goal of winning. More important, such changes encourage individual players to consider their teammates before pursuing an individual course of action. When a player on Coach Goodsport's team begins to act selfishly—by not passing the ball, for instance—the rules of the game (advancement of teammates' positions) require that they think about the other players.

"What does teamwork mean to you?" asks Coach Goodsport.

"Well, not when you are hogging the ball and you are never passing, but when you pass it and you get along with them, that is teamwork."

"How would you have teamwork in baseball?" she continues.

"Well, like when you catch a ball, you might not throw it home when someone has gone home. That is not doing a favor for your team."

❖

Anyone who has attended a ten-and-under soccer game has seen the confusion and lack of teamwork that continues to occur at this age. Players bunch around the ball, concerned with their own goals and neglecting a wider-angle view of the team. The calls for "teamwork" from the sideline may temporarily have the desired effect, but players soon fall back into their self-centered actions. Although frustrating to coaches, it is not surprising that at this age most children still approach sports from an egocentric standpoint. They are focused more on their own interests and concerns than on the needs of the team.

This is a developmental phenomenon and is entirely age appropriate. Teamwork for children at this age is understood more as everyone doing the same thing than as individuals contributing ideas and skills for the betterment of the team. When individual interests conflict with team interests, the young athletes have little understanding of how to move toward a team solution. Yet this age also marks the beginning of the transition from the constraints of Level I to the requirements of more organized competition. This evolution from *me* to *we* gives coaches opportunities to work on the developmental principles and skills necessary to move on to Level III.

Moving Toward the Concept of Team

For many children, this age marks the entry into organized youth sports. But it is also a stage marked by an intense interest in pursuing individual goals. Teamwork and cooperation are understood by children as doing favors for teammates, like throwing the ball to them. Teamwork occurs when the coach or the team members reciprocate with similar favors. Conflicts can arise when a child's interests are not met, because they are not yet able to place the concept of team before their individual interests.

Competition

A competitive game situation can be described as any situation that causes other players to be unable to reach their respective goals. One team's success (winning) interferes with another team's goal (winning). Competitive team sports not only encourage competition *between* teams but often promote the same competitive atmosphere *among* team members when selectivity, performance, and winning are promoted as important goals. If the distribution of positions and playing time, for example, depend on ability and performance (as is the case in many youth sports programs), then the individual players are placed in a situation where their goals—making the team or getting more playing time—are in conflict with those of their teammates. Equity and fairness in this case are based on talent or ability.

When we present winning and extrinsic goals (trophies, team standings, playoffs) to the players as the most important goals, we reinforce qualities such as overcompetitiveness and selfishness. As I stated in Chapter One, I do not think that competition is bad. We need to recognize that it is the basic philosophy of organized competitive sports (no matter how hard we try to proclaim otherwise). The key is to emphasize the positive aspects of sports and competition and not get caught up in inadvertently promoting selfishness, inflated egos, disrespect, and poor sportsmanship.

Restructuring Principles

By restructuring the objectives and rules to include some of the cooperative objectives and rules (such as equal distribution of playing time and positions), competitive sports can be used to promote interdependent goals (such as passing the ball to a teammate in a better position versus hogging the ball). Continue to emphasize skill development and the PLUS core values. These positive life skills can be taught within a competitive sports situation. As youngsters develop skills (physical) and principles (teamwork, fairness, leadership), chances are that they'll win more often in the long run. The idea that teams

■ *Expose Children to a Variety of Sports*

A broad exposure to different sports allows children opportunities to match their interests and abilities and helps ensure that they will not be forced into a sport they do not enjoy. (Except for some specialty sports—gymnastics, swimming, tennis—there is no evidence that early competitive sports are necessary to the later development of the child as an athlete.)

Exposure to a wide variety of sports increases the likelihood that all children will discover an athletic activity that matches their interests and individual talents. Because children develop at different rates, their athletic and personal skills tend to be at different levels, especially during the important growth years. A slender ten-year-old-boy who has not yet grown into his body might not make the football team but might be well suited to be a runner. If given the chance to run track, he could be a top athlete for his age.

that get along well, execute plays well, and work well together will actually win more games is one of the most unrecognized concepts among youth sports coaches.

Continue to use some cooperative games with children at this age. They help young children think about other people's perspectives. Altering competitive team sports to include some of the cooperative objectives and rules such as equal playing time, rotation of positions, and common goals can help young athletes learn to cooperate in competitive situations. Such alterations provide the developmental foundation for understanding collaborative play, which comes later.

Level II Guidelines

Not unlike Level I, children at this age want to play a lot, have fun, and have an encouraging and positive coach. Long and intense activities aimed at developing athletic skills are not likely to be appreciated or understood by many children at the eight- to ten-year-old level. This does not mean coaches shouldn't expect the athletes to work hard and develop skills. Young athletes can work at learning new plays and skills. But you need to be creative when introducing technical drills, keeping it fun. Here are some guidelines for eight- to ten-year-olds. Many of these activities are important at other ages as well, but are especially needed in these years. You'll recognize some from the section about the eight-and-under group.

- **Be Encouraging, Fun, and Supportive**

  From a developmental perspective, eight- to ten-year-olds understand adults more by what they do and how they do it than by what they say. They tend to relate to a situation in very concrete, personal ways. If the coach yells or swears, they may not like him. Kids this age often associate their whole sports experience with how the coach treats them.

  Your major concerns should be for the safety, enjoyment, and confidence of your players. It is important to understand that young children are motivated by adults who are supportive and don't yell. If your children enjoy a certain sport and feel good about themselves, there will be plenty of time to concentrate on specific skills and become more intensely involved later.

- **All Players Share Equal Playing Time**

  The question of how playing time and positions are distributed relates directly to your team philosophy. What have you determined to be most important? What are you trying to accomplish? What do you want your children to learn from playing sports? Eight- to ten-year-old children should enjoy equal playing time and also have the opportunity to play all positions.

  The goal at this age is to develop self-confidence and have fun, not to field the most talented team. Because children develop at different rates physically and athletically, it is difficult to determine who may be the most talented in a few years. By giving the "best" players the prime positions and more playing time, you can create self-fulfilling prophecies. Kids who get the idea early on that they are not as good as their peers begin to believe it to be true. As much fun as sports can be, a nine-year-old who mostly sits on the bench and plays only seven meaningless minutes in a run-away game will soon drop out.

- **Rotate Positions**

  Players should continue to rotate positions to find out where they are comfortable and how well they play in each area. Equally important is seeing the game from different vantage points such as right field, goalie, forward, or first base. This encourages taking different perspectives, which is essential for developing a more mature understanding of teamwork. There will be plenty of time later for specialization and selectivity.

- **Include Different Activities**

  Most successful coaches agree that a diversity of activities decreases the monotony of practices and increases the sense of team spirit. Eight- to ten-year-olds continue to enjoy fun activities (everyone does); when fun is mixed with the necessary skill drills, they are able to sustain their efforts for longer periods of time. Include a variety of fun activities that also provide skill development. Attend a local high school game, play tag or capture the flag, or play a different sport.

To keep her players excited and enthusiastic about practicing, Coach Goodsport concludes every practice with a game that never ends. The players love it because the teams change from practice to practice and no one can quite remember the score or the exact situation where they left off. The focus is on fun and building skills.

Coach Goodsport understands that it is important to engage players in taking responsibility for their own games. She often stands back, offering help when necessary, and encourages her players to design the game strategy and resolve their conflicts themselves.

- **Assign Team and Individual Roles and Responsibilities**

  Try giving team members individual tasks—organize equipment, keep score, keep time, etc. Assigning roles with distinct outcomes builds responsibility and a sense of teamwork.

- **Address and Resolve Conflicts Educationally**

  Conflicts should be mediated quickly and firmly. Keep them under control; think of ways that they can be resolved so that the children learn from the experience. How can the young athletes solve their own problems?

- **Don't Compare Players**

  Don't compare players; this causes hurt feelings and lessens self-confidence.

Summary

You are preparing children at this age for the next level and an increasingly mature understanding of the team concept. Cooperation is still emphasized over competition and should be used to provide opportunities to learn how to work collectively. It is important that your program emphasize the importance of teamwork and deemphasize individual pursuits that do not contribute to the team as a whole. From a developmental perspective, competitive games played cooperatively place the importance of team play before that of individual play.

CHAPTER THIRTEEN

Level III
Ten to Twelve

Eleven-year-old Noah is at an awkward time in his life. His body is changing and so are his interests and friends. For the first time in his life, Noah is thinking of not playing soccer. He had a good time playing on Coach Goodsport's team when he was nine and ten, but sports just don't seem as much fun as they used to be. Noah is developing new interests and new friends. Besides, the soccer league is getting more competitive, and it seems that being highly skilled and winning are getting more important.

Noah is entering the stages of preadolescence when many kids begin to change physically and emotionally and start to question many of the activities and friends they enjoyed just a few years earlier.

The ability to consider one's own and others' perspectives simultaneously is probably one of the most important developmental steps for children. With this capability to "walk in another person's shoes," they are truly able to understand the notion of collaboration. From a developmental standpoint, once children are able to step outside of their own perspective, they are able to understand the team from a "helicopter view," which enables them to place the needs of the team ahead of their individual interests.

Just a few years earlier, the children understood the team as a group of people with separate interests, with each individual negotiating with others to settle claims. Children at Level III understand the team in relation to the sense of togetherness that is achieved when team members have shared interests, goals, and values.

A Developmental Perspective of Team

In these preteen years, young athletes develop the understanding of a team as an integrated whole with common goals. This developmental advance allows players to move beyond the *me* to a collaborative sense of *we*. Delaying personal desires for the sake of the team becomes a meaningful goal. Children at this age also begin to appreciate the diversified role of the coach, becoming more tolerant of a coach who pushes them to advance their skills. The coach brings together common interests in ways that produce team solidarity. The coach should reflect the concerns of the team and promote the team's sense of community. Eleven- and twelve-year-olds describe the following as important aspects of a team:

The Team as a Community

The team as a community, with shared interests and values, is increasingly important. The 11- and 12-year-olds begin to feel that a team where players are close and have similar feelings and ideas is a better team. This notion of *we* becomes the glue that holds a team together.

A Good Team Sticks Together

Central to the notion of team for athletes this age is the idea that all the players, even those who are less skilled, make up the team. A team that sticks together will be a better team.

Everyone Should Contribute in a Meaningful Way

Important point! Two minutes in the last quarter of a runaway game does not provide a player with the feeling that she has contributed to that effort. A team needs all players to contribute and work hard. A player who either doesn't contribute or is neglected affects the whole team.

Friendships Are Increasingly Important

One of the top reasons children play sports is to be with friends. Sharing friendships is an important aspect of being a member of a team. The team is sometimes likened to a family where members are close, know each other well, and are able to work together. In the ideal world, team members would all be friends both on and off the field. This is an unrealistic expectation, but if you stress the PLUS core values, your players will understand and practice respect. Even if certain team members are not friends, they will recognize each other's value and contributions.

Level III Guidelines

Level III is a crucial time for many young athletes. Like Noah, more and more young athletes drop out of sports as a result of selection based on ability, the shift to larger equipment and playing fields, and discrepancies in physical size as a result of differing maturation rates, with some players experiencing an earlier onset of puberty. Young adolescents are also exposed to many changes within their larger social environment; there are adjustments in school, and peer groups exert increasing pressure to conform.

It is important that sports programs offer different opportunities at various ability levels so that developing athletes can compete at their own levels of interest and competence. The following guidelines are especially important in making the sports experience positive for preteens.

- **Teach Important Life Skills**

   As children mature intellectually, physically, and socially, they are more capable of enjoying competitive games with a focus on winning as a process and product. They can now balance the demands of navigating within a competitive social situation with a developmentally more mature understanding of what competition actually means. With their increased interest in the team as a close unit, competition can help them understand achievement, collaborative effort, and collective responsibility.

   Striving to win, with winning equated with achievement and skill mastery, can be a way of learning the value of individual team members' contribution of different skills and ideas to the team as a whole. You can help your athletes understand more developed ideas of how they can work together as a team by consoling teammates, working out conflicts, taking on their individual responsibilities as team members, and so on.

- **Increase Skill Instruction**

   Although skill instruction is important for eight- to ten-year-olds, the emphasis is still more on fun. Eleven- and twelve-year-olds have longer attention spans and greater motivation to learn the technical aspects of the game. In general, between the ages of ten and thirteen, children understand the long-term value of learning the skills for an activity. Although fun is still important, older athletes are learning the importance of practicing longer to perfect their skills. They are also learning the connection of the skills with the overall structure of the sport.

- **Emphasize Continuous Improvement and Skill Mastery**

   Young athletes at this age learn that hard work and discipline lead to continuous improvement and success. It is important to help players understand the value of perseverance in the face of difficulty and the value of hard work. The athlete who understands

that a missed grounder is a mistake that can be learned from is more likely to keep trying than the athlete who sees a mistake as the result of natural ability (or lack of it). For example, Gordon Goodsport is not the gifted athlete that Tommy Too-Cool is, but Gordon understands that sustained effort leads to continuous improvement. Tommy on the other hand, has not yet made the connection, and mistakes such as striking out only frustrate him.

Older athletes increasingly value coaches who teach skills. Athletes appreciate practices that focus more on learning the correct way to perform a particular skill and less on simply having fun. Remember the seven-year-olds who like coaches who are "nice"? For seven-year-olds, a good coach is someone who "does things for us." Children over ten are developing a more diversified notion of a good coach that includes someone who teaches skills as well as someone who understands them.

- **Promote Teamwork Through Shared Experiences**

  Preteens are preoccupied with peers and what their friends think and feel. They want and need to be accepted. Many athletes this age prefer that team members have similar ideas and goals to make the team a shared experience. Personal and team goals such as giving one's best and caring about other team members' thoughts and feelings are important to keep the team united and striving for mutual goals. Not all teams share close feelings and expectations. Because teams are made up of individual players with different interests, subgroups that can disrupt this sense of closeness sometimes form. You need to be aware that this happens frequently and work to minimize its effects on the team.

- **Promote Leadership Opportunities**

  Eleven- and twelve-year-olds can serve as role models for younger players. They can help coach younger children, umpire and officiate at games, and help organize practices. This is good experience for both younger and older children. Help your players find opportunities to develop their leadership skills and offer them guidance and supervision.

  These opportunities are particularly important for this age group, because this is when many young athletes stop playing organized team sports. Even if they no longer play a sport, they can plan practices and teach skills, with the guidance and mentoring of an older coach. The younger coaches take this responsibility and accountability seriously. Developing leadership skills also provides players with meaningful sports-related experience they can use in other areas of their lives, such as being counselors at a summer camp.

- **Demanding and Understanding: Find the Balance**

  Young athletes at this age want to be challenged and train hard, but at the same time they want a balanced environment that mixes work with an understanding of the need of adolescents to be part of the decision-making process. As children enter adolescence they tend to be moody and may not always mean what they say or do; sometimes they'll say they are tired and don't want to practice, but later will thank you for a good work-out.

  Adolescents want and need to be understood. If they feel the coach hears and understands them, they will work harder than they will for a coach who doesn't care or appears not to care. Though they may not show it, adolescents notice the attention a coach gives them. Your sports program should be organized to include opportunities for the athletes to share their feelings and thoughts.

- **Dialogue with Athletes**

  This is probably the most overlooked opportunity for promoting growth. Adults often forget the importance of building relationships. Many children today do not have adults they can talk with.

Kids want and need adults they can bounce ideas off and share their feelings with. Use Warm-Up and Cool-Down sessions to talk with your players about what's on their minds. This builds trust and understanding; when an issue arises during a game, there is a relationship in place. Simply talking with your team with no goal in mind can have an incredible impact on the overall feeling of the team.

- **Listen to Their Ideas**

  It is important to try to understand and appreciate the thoughts of your athletes even though you may not agree with them or plan to use them. Young adolescents enjoy the opportunity to engage in team decision making. You can create situations where the team chooses sides, rotates positions, and runs the Warm-Up and Cool-Down sessions. Empowering players to take responsibility for their ideas contributes to their growth as people and as athletes.

  What if one day you said to your team, "OK, there is the equipment. I want you to take the next hour to prepare for our game on Saturday." Would your team know what to do? Have you prepared them to take responsibility, or do they need you in order to make decisions? Individual and group discussions are a great educational medium to teach critical thinking. Remember— the most important part of talking can be listening. When we really listen to and respect our athletes, they buy into our values.

- **Help Athletes Set Realistic Athletic Goals**

  What are individual players' strengths? What is important to them? Is there a chance a player might compete in high school? It is important to help athletes find appropriate sports opportunities based on experience, ability, and other commitments.

Summary

This can be an interesting time for coaches working with this age group. Children ten to twelve are undergoing a lot of changes, and many of them, especially those who have been playing a sport for a number of years, may be ready for an increase in the intensity of competition. They are also looking to increase their skill level in preparation for playing on higher level teams in middle school and high school. But this is also the age at which a number of children drop out of youth sports, even though their past experiences may be positive.

It is important for coaches to recognize where individual children may be within this spectrum, what they need to continue, or what sort of involvement in sports those ready to drop out might be interested in. The principles and structure of the PLUS model continue to work, however, regardless of the age level and intensity of competition. Just because winning, tournaments, playing time, and competition move up a notch doesn't mean that children can not continue developing positive character values and further their personal development through their sports experiences.

Beyond the Playing Fields

There is a lot of attention currently being paid to issues involving youth sports—the competitive nature of sports themselves; the positive and negative aspects of winning and losing; the emphasis placed by our society on being a "winner." How these issues are understood and debated, and which side you take, will greatly effect the sports experience you present.

Many children who participate in youth sports programs will not go on to play on a high school team. Most will not go on to compete at the collegiate level, and fewer still will ever play professionally. So what lessons can and should children take with them from their first sports experiences? What examples from their competitive games can be transferred to a child's life away from sports— to community, to school, and to family? Sports provide many opportunities to learn to be a responsible and contributing member of a community.

CHAPTER FOURTEEN

Fun, Winning, and Other Myths

Whenever I talk with someone about the PLUS model, they usually respond with what turns out to be their personal philosophy of sports and life. I guess I shouldn't be surprised. Everyone has a theory, usually based on their personal experience. In the case of youth sports, it seems that there are many experts and many opinions. My point is that I think it is important for those of us involved with children in sports to be clear on what we believe. In order to do this, we need to examine some of the widely held myths surrounding youth sports.

Sports Are Positive for Everyone

The first myth is that sports are actually good for everyone. In theory, sports could and should be good for everyone. In reality, we all know that this is not always true. The quality of the sports experience rests heavily on the coach's philosophy and how that philosophy is put into practice. If we believe that sports should be positive for everyone, then coaches need to develop a philosophy and set of values to follow that ensures the sports experience will be positive for *all* children. It is especially important to create an environment that not only accepts but actively encourages those children who are at a greater risk of having a negative experience.

These children are usually the ones that are shy, sensitive, not naturally athletic, sometimes overweight, and, sometimes, girls. What I mean by not only accepting but encouraging is that simply saying that everyone will share equal playing time is only a start. Do we have enough confidence to back up our beliefs by putting a weaker player in the game when winning is at stake? Do we covertly reward the better players with the way we talk to them and act with them? Do we inadvertently send messages to the girls on the team that they are not as good as the boys?

The point I am trying to make is the same one that I have stated throughout this book: whether sports are good for everyone has a great deal to do with the type of environment you as the coach create. At the Sports PLUS

Camp we have developed a culture that believes in and rewards all players equally as people and as atheletes. Young children pick up early on what we believe. If we really want to debunk the myth that sports are only positive for the better players, then we need to create an environment that supports our beliefs.

Do Sports Build Character or Characters?

By now we understand that sports in and of themselves do not guarantee positive character development. The Sports PLUS model has outlined in detail the preconditions necessary to encourage players to learn to be respectful and responsible teammates and citizens. If sports are designed to include an integrated philosophy and psychology that is sensitive to how children learn and includes the appropriate activities, such as opportunities for positive modeling and dialogue, then the core values can and will be developed. The best way to assure that sports build character is to take a proactive approach in designing your youth sports program.

Fun Is More Important Than Winning

Probably the most common response I get when I talk about youth sports is that sports for children should be fun. Most of these comments go on to say that we place too much emphasis on winning and competition. Some people even go so far as to say that competition is damaging to our children and we should not introduce them to competitive activities like organized youth sports. On the other side of the fun/competition debate are those who say that competition is a natural part of life and we should prepare our children for the challenges that life naturally presents. To further explore this debate, let's begin by looking at why winning is valued within our society.

Why Winning Is Valued

The media glamorizes the importance, glory, and excitement of winning. In fact, it is through the media that most young children first become exposed to the professional sports world. But overemphasis on winning can and often does lead to detrimental effects on children.

Too often coaches and parents of children playing sports forget that the goals of youth sports are different from those of professional sports. Younger athletes are not earning a living as athletes, nor will many of them go on to do so, despite the aspirations of their parents. Coaches and parents both need to help young athletes understand the difference between professional sports and youth sports. Perhaps as importantly, coaches often need to help parents understand the difference, as obvious as it may seem.

We are often so concerned with what we want our children to become that we forget what they are and need to be right now: children.

Besides being fun, winning is often seen as a way of measuring one's self-worth. Many coaches, perhaps as a way of reliving their own sports experiences, let their egos get in the way of their concern for the children's personal growth. They get caught up, often without realizing it, with emphasizing the end product more than the process of getting there. Regardless of what they say, they place all or most of their emphasis on winning. This sets children up with one goal—winning. When they don't win, they fail.

Another problem is that when winning is stressed as the most desired outcome, most behaviors that lead to winning become acceptable. Young children are not developed enough to understand the complexity of the relationship between competitive sports at higher levels and youth sports. For instance, an eight-year-old boy watching a professional hockey player slam an opponent into the deck can't understand why he shouldn't do the same thing to his opponents.

There are a couple of potentially harmful things that can develop out of a winning-is-the-only-thing mentality. One is that children become motivated more by extrinsic rewards than by performance and goals. Ultimately, children may lose motivation if the rewards are not there. Another is that a young athlete may compete at such an early age and at such an intense pace that he may burn out before fully developing his potential.

Dangers of Early Competition

Much is made of the problems of overemphasizing competition, early specialization, and stress. Although these are real concerns, I don't think that competition in and of itself is at the root of the problem. The key here is to remember the many benefits of youth sports. If organized as I have outlined throughout this book, competitive sports can and do teach children to work together on a team, be respectful of both teammates and opponents, take responsibility for their actions, engage in fair play, and persevere when faced with challenges. All of these benefits play into the larger arena of self-esteem. As children understand their goals, immerse themselves in challenges, and are offered opportunities for discussion and reflection, a positive sense of self can emerge. In this way, competition advances our goal of using sports for a positive learning experience.

But what about the very real negative effects of competition? This is a very important question. Excessive competition can lead to loss of self-esteem, low achievement motivation, and lack of interest in further participation in sports. It is sad to think that an activity designed for kids to have fun and feel good about themselves would ever do just the opposite.

Some sports models suggest changes in intensity, rules, and competitive levels, but often without saying when and how these changes should be made. Many claims are made either by researchers who are unfamiliar with sports or by sports researchers extrapolating from research done in other settings, such as a clinic or a classroom. On the other side of the debate are those who feel

■ *Learning Negative Values*

Certainly one of the worst dangers of early specialization and overly intense competition is the creation of egotistical child-athletes. We have all seen these young prima donnas who feel that the world in general, and parents, coaches, and teammates in particular, owe them a living. They need (and usually have) the best equipment, want to play the most, and talk constantly about their stellar performances. They are seldom team players. When the team loses, they blame the loss on their teammates and care more about how they played themselves.

Developmental psychology warns of us of the potential danger of allowing young children to bask solely in the glory of their performances. Unfortunately, our society often seems to favor competition over cooperation. Children learn at an early age that it is more prized socially to win or beat another person than it is to cooperate. Encouraging young children to compare themselves to others through overly competitive situations can result in self-centered children who later have trouble adjusting. Children should be judged against their individual goals, not against other children.

that too much is made of deemphasizing intensity, competition, and winning. This is also unsettling. The fact is, there is little empirical evidence showing that competition and striving to win are in and of themselves detrimental to children's development.

The critical point is that if a coach who can offer proper reinforcement and discussion introduces competition at the appropriate age, in the context of personal achievement, and in a positive learning environment, then competition can be beneficial to a child's overall development.

So, Should Young Children Compete?

Yes. I believe that to avoid competition entirely is to deny children opportunities to grow through both disappointment and success. A sports environment that introduces competition at the right time and as a process and product can help children begin to prepare for many of the challenges they will face in school, in the community, and in the work world.

Competition in youth sports programs is such a hotly debated topic because we have become so obsessed with winning and losing that we have lost sight of the process—the striving for excellence, the pushing to reach new goals and break through perceived limitations. If we look at competition as a chance to better ourselves at something, then the end result—win or lose—becomes less important. All the things achieved or learned in preparing for the contest are not lost, but serve to make us better than we were.

Play Different Sports

My last point is that sports should be structured so that children can explore a variety of interests. This is a time for children to try out various sports to find one that matches their abilities and interests. If a child enjoys a certain sport and feels good about herself, there will be plenty of time to become more intensely involved later.

Exposure to a wide variety of sports also allows young children to develop diverse skills and interests. Although most people don't continue team sports beyond high school or college, activities such as swimming, running, tennis, and skiing are enjoyed by people of all ages. The most important thing is for children to have positive sports experiences early. Even if they eventually quit a particular sport, developing an interest in physical activities is important to an overall healthy life.

Summary

Many adults desperately want their sons and daughters to be *winners*. They think they need to push hard to get a jump on the competition. While this may be true in some specialty sports such as gymnastics or tennis, there is no indication that early competitive sports exposure gives children much of an advantage later. In most cases, young children need a time when their activity is simply fun and they get to be with their friends.

The most important thing during this early period is to build the motivational foundation for the future. When we maintain a healthy sense of competition and show a sense of proportion about winning, our children will learn the positive values associated with striving to do their best, develop self-confidence, and transfer what they learn to other areas of their lives.

CHAPTER FIFTEEN

Beyond the Playing Field

Can sports help teach children how to be responsible and productive members of their communities? What role, if any, do sports play in our schools? Besides the physical benefits, such as the development of basic motor skills and physical fitness, sports and physical education contribute to the cognitive, social, moral, and emotional needs of the child—the whole person. Through sports, we can develop creative and divergent thinking skills. We can promote understanding and lessen the fear of people who are different. We can learn how to manage our emotions and practice self-discipline. We can learn to compromise, solve problems, and resolve conflicts.

This last chapter builds on the power of organized sports but widens its focus to include an expanded array of ways sports can be used for positive learning. One of the PLUS principles is the transference of the values we learn in sports to other important areas of life—school, community, and home. The saying that it takes an entire community to raise a child takes on added significance when we think about developing our players' character beyond the playing fields.

Our respective towns and community members expend a great deal of resources, including time, energy, and money, into making sure our children have opportunities to participate in sports programs. It is important for children to understand what this effort means and the value of service to others. As in the scenario in Chapter One, when Coach Goodsport reminded her team to show appreciation for their opponents, our young players need to appreciate what our communities do for them.

Sports in Our Community

The community gives to our children in many ways. Our children are provided with playing fields, uniforms, umpires, and coaches. The young athletes should learn to give back to their communities as contributing and responsible citizens. As a way to encourage service to others as well as an appreciation for all the community does for her team, Coach Goodsport engages her team in community service projects like raking leaves for elderly residents, volunteering to help younger children learn to play soccer, and helping to keep their own playing fields in good condition.

Beyond the benefits gained by helping others, Coach Goodsport also develops stronger bonds with her team and takes the children's learning process to a new level. The children on her team understand how to put the lessons learned playing soccer to use in their daily lives. They are learning to think of others in need and how they can help. These are powerful lessons for young children to learn; the more they begin to think about their roles in their communities, the more they start to consider their roles in other areas of their lives.

Sports in the Classroom

This year an estimated 35 million children and adolescents will participate in organized youth sports. Surprisingly, however, there will be little or no connection between the young athletes' sports experiences and their experiences in the classroom. Yet, as we have seen throughout this book, sports can be a powerful tool for teaching and learning. Children's experiences and involvement in sports can increase literacy and strengthen positive values and interpersonal skills. Sports motivate many children and offer concrete experiences from which real learning can evolve.

A Case for Sports

One reason that educators are reluctant to include sports in the school curriculum is that sports and physical education are viewed as primarily physical activities. Educators have neglected or failed to acknowledge the cognitive, emotional, social, and moral aspects. Another reason is that we tend to view people, like sports, in narrow terms. Despite the current interest in holistic approaches, the image of the person as composed of two parts—mind and body—remains strong. Within this framework, the body (physical half) is viewed as inferior or less important than the mind (intellectual half). This is reflected in the fact that sports and physical education are considered "extra-curricular" activities (literally outside the curriculum). School curricula are built around mental and physical distinctions. For example, in language arts we do reading and writing; in physical education class, we do movement activities and games.

Integrating sports into the curriculum first requires an understanding that sports are valuable—more than a physical activity or form of entertainment. Secondly, we need to recognize that all children learn through the games they play and watch.

Learning Through Sports

Based on the theoretical view that children are meaning makers and learn by linking new information to prior knowledge or experiences, instruction should encourage children to use what they already know. Good teaching should build on students' personal strengths. Too often, though, the focus is on what children do not know.

Abstract concepts like teamwork and fair play are difficult, especially for elementary students. These "big ideas" are better explained and illustrated using examples, experiences, and language with which children are familiar. Viewed in this context, the sports metaphor becomes a powerful teacher. By linking the familiar to the unfamiliar, metaphors can help us see relationships. The sports metaphor can help children extend their understanding to other situations in life. For example, children can learn how playing fair in a game relates to playing fair in school and in life in general.

What's more, sports is a subject that engages children. Sports speak to issues children care about: universal issues such as justice, discrimination, and respect. Learning is more meaningful, relevant, and fun when it occurs in a context children can relate to. John Dewey understood this when he said, "Experience is most rewarding when it involves the seemingly contradictory traits of rigor and playfulness."

The School PLUS Program

The School PLUS program grew out of early successes incorporating sports literature in our summer sports camps. We were amazed that children were not only reading in the summer, but wanted to read. Campers read for enjoyment and for information. They also learned about teamwork, respect, and responsibility—values we encouraged on the playing fields. With the poor reading levels of elementary school children, coupled with the sharp increase in youth violence, we saw great potential in bringing the sports experience into the classroom.

The goals of School PLUS are to teach interpersonal skills, promote reading and language development, and build self-esteem. It is organized around the five Sports PLUS themes—teamwork, respect, responsibility, fair play, and perseverance. Lessons integrate reading, writing, speaking, and thinking skills into the subject of sports. Students explore the curriculum in a number of ways, including dialogue and discussion, cooperative teams, role playing, journal writing, webs, brainstorming, and, of course, sports. By offering a variety of learning experiences, we are able to address children's multiple intelligences such as kinesthetic, visual, verbal, and auditory learning. Most importantly, we are able to engage all children in at least some of the activities.

The program is unique in that students not only play sports, but also study how sports relate to their lives. Students explore such complex issues as discrimination, justice, and violence. Learning objectives emphasize three interrelated areas:

1. **Language Skills:** Participate and express oneself in group discussions, develop an interest and appreciation for reading, respond to literature both orally and in writing, develop listening skills, build reading comprehension skills, interpret literary themes and their implications.

2. **Thinking Skills:** Understand cause-and-effect relationships, predict outcomes and draw conclusions, interpret motives, make comparisons and contrasts, think of alternative solutions to problems.

3. **Interpersonal Skills and Values:** Develop perspective-taking and empathy skills, manage feelings, respond appropriately to conflict, cooperate and work in small teams, develop a greater understanding and acceptance of others.

Emphasizing skill development in these three areas ensures that the program is integrated and helps meet both the cognitive and affective needs of children.

Intended Audience

School PLUS targets both girls and boys in grades four through six. The program is not just for children who play sports but also for the many kids who have never played on an organized team. The program concentrates on this age group for the following reasons:

- Early intervention is likely to be more effective.
- Age ten marks the highest rate for participation in team sports.
- Early adolescents begin to spend significant amounts of time in the company of peers.
- Children at this age develop a greater capacity for abstract thinking.

The program is of particular importance to economically disadvantaged children and young adolescent girls. Because the cost for participation in youth sports has risen dramatically during the past several years, many children, especially those living in inner-city neighborhoods, are denied equal opportunity to play.

Although women's sports participation has increased sixfold in the last 20 years, many girls are still discouraged from participation. In School PLUS, girls learn they can be competent players who can take risks, meet challenges, and most importantly have fun. For example, in *Wilma Unlimited*, by Kathleen Krull, students learn of the courage and determination of Olympic track star Wilma Rudolph. Nikia, a fourth-grade participant in 1995, explained, "I learned that if you don't try you don't know if you can do something. It helped me work better with people and give everybody a chance."

Program Setting

With its emphasis on reading, discussion, and sports, School PLUS can be implemented into language arts and reading programs, youth sports programs, recreation centers, and libraries; however, we see the after-school setting as the area of greatest need. For most children, there are few choices after school. Many children spend their time watching television or engaging in risky behavior. Thirty percent of fifth graders go home every afternoon to an empty house, according to a Carnegie Foundation survey. And nearly two-thirds said they wish they had more things to do. The children who most need access to quality after-school programs are those living in inner-city neighborhoods. While 71% of high-income families offer after-school activities for kids 11–14, only 20% of low-income neighborhoods offer the same service (*Inside ED*, January 15, 1995).

Early Results

In 1995–1996, School PLUS was piloted at a Boston elementary school as an after-school program. It served 24 fourth- and fifth-grade Chapter I boys and girls. The program met three days a week for about two hours. Staff and students collaborated on daily and weekly schedules that included time for classroom-based activities, such as reading a book or role playing a social situation, and sports, such as three-on-three basketball or whiffle ball. Early results were encouraging:

- Students increased the time they spent on reading both in and out of class.

- Pre- and post- surveys showed a growth in students' understanding of the program's themes—teamwork, respect, responsibility, fair play, and perseverance.

- Students improved their ability to work and play in small teams.

How the children received the program is perhaps the best measure of the program's overall success. Attendance was over 98% (this is significant given that attendance was voluntary). We found that both boys and girls, whether or not they had played sports, were motivated to read, write, and participate in class discussions. "Kids can learn how to set goals without cheating or hurting someone. You also learn teamwork, responsibility, and a lot of respect. I would like it if the after-school program would be longer," commented Jonathan, a ten-year-old participant.

Curriculum Components

Literature serves as the major instructional medium. For example, Matt Christopher's *The Hit-Away Kid* is one book used in the fair play unit. On a fly ball to left field, Barry McGee, the "Hit-Away Kid," appears to make a great catch in left field. While the umpire calls the batter out, Barry knows he dropped the ball. Barry must decide what is more important—playing by the rules or playing to win. Students respond and react to personal experiences and what they read, chart progress, and set goals in their own journals, called the *Sports Ledger*.

Additional activities include:

- Sports vignettes created to promote dialogue and discussion

- Sports dilemmas in which children explore consequences and generate alternative courses of action

- Sports cartoons that challenge children to determine what the characters are thinking and feeling

- Current events

- A quote of the day

Students build on the lessons learned in the classroom by participating in a variety of sports and cooperative games. Visits from athletes and other professionals add another exciting dimension to the program. By talking about the program's themes, reading with the children, and participating in activities, these individuals serve as important role models.

Instructional Approach

Coaching is an excellent analogy—first, the coach psyches her players up and gets them ready before a practice or a game. She explains and models skills and sets goals with the team. Next, the players go out on the field and practice. During practice the coach provides feedback and encouragement. After practice, the coach huddles the team up to discuss and reflect upon what happened and how they played.

These three processes, the Warm-Up, Activity, and Cool-Down, make up the instructional framework of School PLUS. The teacher's role is that of a coach, facilitator, and problem poser. This is quite different from the traditional didactic method in which the adult assumes center stage. In contrast to traditional classrooms, the student is the prime actor, rather than the passive spectator. In keeping with the Socratic tradition, students are asked to examine and grapple with ideas and experiences and to apply their knowledge in different situations. In short, children are given real responsibility for their own learning.

The Cool-Down provides the best opportunity for children to reflect on what they are learning (content) as well as how they are learning (process). During this time children are also encouraged to make connections among themes and to their own lives. The students at the Sarah Greenwood School in Dorchester, Massachusetts, for example, read and discussed Dean Hughes' book *One Man Team*. In this story, eighth-grader Aaron Reeves has trouble making friends on his new basketball team. Although he is the most talented player on the team, the coach thinks he is a ball hog and the players think he is a showoff. Students explored the idea of teamwork in depth. They discussed what it means to be a team player and were invited to share stories of teammates in their own lives. The qualities of a good teammate were discussed in the context of the life of the classroom as well as the court. "Don't be like Reeves!" was often shouted out as the children played basketball in the school lot. Issues such inclusion, friendship, and selfish play were discussed with great interest.

Sports PLUS at Home

Values such as teamwork, respect, and responsibility learned on the playing field are valuable at home as our children interact with their siblings and conduct their chores. Over the years I have received many letters from parents saying that their child has developed a more respectful relationship with a brother or sister as a result of the respectful relationships at the Sports PLUS Camp.

Sometimes it is easier for parents to reiterate what the coach says is important than to have to continually nag. It is also helpful if our children actually initiate respectful behavior because that is what is expected on their team. In this case, as parents we can simply sit back and support these positive behaviors. The respect and responsibility scales outlined in Chapter Four are excellent guidelines for understanding responsibilities around the house. One way to begin this process is to discuss with children what their responsibilities are.

Once you come to an understanding, you can plug in the leader-to-detractor scale for responsibility. Be sure to include concrete behaviors at each level so children understand the goals and where their current behaviors fit on the scale.

The scales represent actual behaviors and can be adapted to reflect family responsibilities. For example, if your child's chores include taking out the trash or cleaning, then parents and children have a goal, five levels of observable behaviors, and a measuring device. If the child takes out the trash only when we ask her, she is at level two of responsibility. If she not only understands her role as a family member but asks for additional opportunities to contribute to the family, then she is at level four and is a contributor. Just as on the playing field, be sure to make this fun. Discuss with children actual behaviors rather than using general terms like "you need to be more responsible!" The most important idea is that the lessons that children learn on the playing field can be transferred to other areas of life.

Summary

In addition to their tremendous motivational appeal, sports provide rich and exciting subject matter for helping children understand life's challenges and responsibilities. Research on resilient children—children who "beat the odds"—points to several common characteristics these children share: social competence, problem-solving skills, close social bonds, and a sense of purpose and hope for the future. If properly structured, sports and physical education can work to support many of these protective factors.

The idea that sports can promote positive values is not new. Through positive role models and a well-thought-out philosophy, youth sports programs can teach children important life lessons. What is novel, and the focus of this last chapter, is the notion of capturing and making the most of children's natural interest in sports. Sports are everywhere in our children's lives: at school, at the mall, and at home. Our children are watching sports on TV and reading about their heroes in the papers. Sports provide powerful lessons that naturally arise from action and provide us with a powerful teaching tool.

When the whole community, including coaches, teachers, and parents, joins the process of educating the whole child, the likelihood that positive learning will occur increases. "It takes a village to raise a child" is transformed from a catchy phrase into a meaningful lifelong experience.

Appendix I

Sample Letter to Parents

Dear Parents,

Welcome to another season! I am looking forward to the challenges of coaching your child's team and hope that we all will have fun and enjoy the experience. I would like to give you a brief introduction to my coaching philosophy and acquaint you with my goals for the team.

I will be following the guidelines of a program called PLUS—positive learning using sports. This model stresses the positive benefits of sports by building a team environment in which all the children feel safe, both physically and emotionally. This program also incorporates five character values—responsibility, respect, teamwork, fair play and perseverance—which children can be taught to recognize through the action of sports.

The structure of the program uses a cycle of Warm-Up—a brief meeting before every practice and game in which the team discusses skill and value related goals and issues; the Activity—game or practice from which the team identifies specific actions that represent the values we identify and goals we set, both team and individual; the Cool-Down—a post-game or practice meeting where we again discuss how we did as a team in working toward our goals.

Because of this structure, it is important that players arrive for games at least twenty minutes before game time. It will also be helpful if your child can plan to stay for a few minutes after each game for our Cool-Down.

As far as my philosophy toward winning and competition, I believe that children at this age need to develop a positive and healthy competitive attitude that is based on individual performance and success. I try to instill in the children a sense of intrinsic motivation rather than a reliance on extrinsic rewards. Both team and individual goals will stress continuous improvement, skill development, and maintaining a positive attitude. Winning will be discussed within the context of our performance as a team, not as a priority. By placing winning (and losing) within the process of the game, we will emphasize our performance based on how well we execute the skills we work on in practice and on how well we achieve our goals. I believe that the process of competing, practicing and improving on skills, and of achieving incremental goals is more important than the end result. The interesting thing about this approach is that by de-emphasizing winning over the process, winning takes care of itself and the team usually has a great deal of success.

My ultimate goal for the children on my team is that they all have a positive experience, have fun (the number one reason why children play sports in the first place), and develop self-esteem and self-confidence. Playing time and positions will be equally distributed.

I share this information with you because I think it is important that you understand my philosophy and goals for our team. I also think it is important that you are able to discuss with your child the values and ideals that I will be teaching through their sports experience. If you have any questions or concerns please do not hesitate to talk to me.

Parent's Questionnaire

Why I think my child wants to play on a sports team.

_____

_____

_____

Why I want him/her to play on a sports team.

_____

_____

_____

What I think his/her goals should be.

_____

_____

_____

What my goals are.

_____

_____

_____

What I want the coach to teach.

_____

_____

_____

What I want my child to learn from her/his sports experience.

_____

_____

_____

Appendix II

On the following pages you will find a number of cooperative games from Project Adventure that work well with youth sports teams. All of these activities are high in fun but also serve to teach cooperation, game strategy, and quick thinking. They can be used early in a season to set a tone of fun and working together as a group and at any other point during the season to break up skill drills or stress cooperation and teamwork. All of the activities came from Project Adventure's *Youth Leadership In Action* and *QuickSilver*, both of which are listed at the end of this book.

■ Impulse

This activity is a good one to use early on in a season or if you haven't been together for a while. It can be used to introduce goal setting or just as a way for your team to reconnect.

How to Play

- Get the group in a circle and have everyone hold hands with the people beside them. Choose a starting person.
- Have the starter squeeze the hands of a player whose hand they are holding. That child (the one who received the squeeze) squeezes the hand of the next person and so on. This hand squeezing continues so that the *Impulse* goes around the circle until it gets back to the player who started it.

Other Ideas

- Have the group pick a goal for the amount of time it might take for the *Impulse* to go around the circle. Try to help them find a goal that everyone can agree on.
- Try sending the *Impulse* in a different direction from the first time you went around.
- Have the group try it with their eyes close—is it any harder or slower?
- Try it with a new starting player.
- Try sending an *Impulse* in both directions at the same time by having the starter squeeze both hands at the same time. The *Impulse* will cross somewhere near the halfway point of the circle and both *Impulses* should get back to the starter (should is a key word here). Give the group a few tries if they lose an *Impulse* somewhere along the way.

■ Monarch

This is another good warm-up activity that gets the children moving. It also is a good game for changing roles and for teaching children strategy and the importance of being in position to get a pass from another player.

How to Play

The Monarch (the *It* person) starts off with a ball—a Nerf-type ball works best because you want it to be something that throws well but that a child won't mind getting hit with. DO NOT use soccer balls, tennis balls, or anything else that might hurt if a player gets hit in the head by it. Choose a Monarch to begin the activity. This person tries to hit an Anarchist (anybody else) with the ball. If hit, a child becomes a Monarch and then helps the other Monarchs turn more Anarchists to their side.

Rules

Establish boundaries that leave room for lots of running but that also allows the Monarch a fair chance of catching someone. If an Anarchists run out of bounds, they become a Monarch.

Once there are two Monarchs (or three or four depending on the age of your players), Monarchs cannot run if they have the ball. They can only throw it or pass it to another Monarch. (If they drop or miss a pass, usually with young children, they can retrieve the ball but then cannot move.) This is where strategy and positioning is important.

■ Moonball

Moonball is a classic cooperative activity because of its guaranteed fun-factor. It works well with kids of all ages and with any size group. It can be played indoors or outdoors, just as long as you have a pretty large playing area, like a gym.

Things You'll Need

One or more beach balls

How to Play

Explain to the players that their objective is to see how many times they can hit the ball into the air without letting it hit the ground. Once the ball hits the ground the count starts again at zero. The only other rules are that the beach ball must be hit with hands only (see variations) and that it can't be hit by the same person two times in a row.

Things to Think About

This is another activity where goal setting can be talked about and tried. You may want to give the team a trial run to see how well they do. Once they have done this, you can have them establish a team goal, like how many hits they think they'll get before the ball hits the ground. Give them several attempts to reach this goal and once they have made it, see if they'd like to go for more.

■ Safety Note

Do not allow kicking the ball. A high kicking foot becomes a real safety problem for other players.

Be sure that all the players are involved and that a few don't take over. Have a rule that all team members must hit the ball before any one can hit it a second time.

Many times, right after the ball hits the ground, someone will pick it up and hit it to start a new attempt. If this happens over and over again, you may want to step in and give them a two-minute time-out for planning. Give the kids time to plan some strategies. During a Cool-Down (at the end of the activity or end of practice), ask them if they stopped to think things through. Children will often get caught up in working *harder* when working *smarter* was what was actually needed. A good lesson.

After a few tries you can begin adding two points for a *header* — hitting the ball with your head instead of your hands.

■ Quick Line-Up

Quick Line-Up is a very fun, action-oriented, team-building activity. You'll want to be in a gym, large room or field for this one because of the fast action. It's a great activity to use with young children to begin teaching them that a playing field has different positions or zones. Have a soccer team dribble their balls from one position to the other.

How to Play

- The leader has the group form a square with an equal number of people on each of the four sides (or as close to an equal number as possible). Players should be standing close together and facing the inside of the square. The leader is in the middle and is facing one of the four sides of the square.

- Each side of the square represents a team, therefore there are four teams.

- For the first part of the activity, all players in the square need to remember who is on their right and who is on their left (the end players only have to remember the person next to them who is on their team, they don't need to worry about the person on the other team). Give the group ten seconds to check out who is beside them—if it's a group whose members don't know each other well, give them a minute and have players introduce themselves to their teammates.

- The *teams* must also remember how they are lined up in relation to the leader who is in the middle of the square. As the leader you want to make it very obvious which way you are facing—no angles or anything, just straight on so that one team is directly in front of you, one is on your left, one on your right and one team is directly behind you. With young children, hold something in one of your hands so they don't get mixed up with right and left.

- Now that you are all set up, the game goes like this: You (the leader) spin around in the middle of the square and stop, facing a new direction. When you stop, yell, "Quick Line-Up!"

- Each team must now line up on the same side of you that they began on. For example, the team that started behind you has to be behind you again; the team that started on your left has to be directly on your left; etc.

- Not only does each team have to line up in relation to you, but the players on each team must also be lined up in the same exact order as they were to begin with.

- When a group is in the right place, and all of its team members are lined up in the right order, they need to join hands and yell, "Quick Line-Up" while lifting their hands into the air.

■ *Safety issues:*

As always, the safety of everyone in the group is shared between you and the group. If you feel an accident is possible because of the way anyone or group is acting, you need to either talk with them about it right then or stop the activity.

If your kids are really wound up, use a no running rule.

■ Speed Rabbit

This activity is a lot of fun but also works on cognitive skills. It also has different players working together in always changing groups.

How to Play

- Have your team form a circle.

- Choose one person to be in the center of the circle. When you first introduce the activity, take this position yourself.

- As the leader, turn around and around, and randomly stop and point to someone and call out a character. (See below for some characters to use.)

- The player pointed to is the main body of the character, and the people that are on each side of this player are the two sides.

- The leader counts to ten, fast or slow, and if the three people creating the character haven't completed it by the time the leader reaches ten, or if a child makes the wrong movement, the person pointed to (the *body*) or the one making the mistake replaces the leader in the center of the circle. The old leader joins the circle with the other players.

- Start by demonstrating the different characters. Three choices are usually enough to remember but you can add a fourth or fifth later on. Let the kids create the new ones.

Other Ideas

If you have a large group, try two players in the center of the circle both pointing and calling out characters.

A fun way to end the game is to have leaders stay in the center when people goof up or don't get done quickly enough. Since the person pointed to comes into the circle when this happens, there will now be two leaders in the middle who can call on any unsuspecting trio. As players make mistakes, they come into the middle, but the old ones stay there, too. By doing this, the number of people in the middle grows and grows until there's no one left outside.

Ideas for Characters

Rabbit—The middle child brings his hands up to his face and wiggles his fingers like whiskers, or puts his hands up behind his head as ears. The children to each side stomp a foot up and down.

Elephant—The person in the middle holds one arm out in front of their nose making the trunk. The children on each side form ears by bringing their outside arms out and placing a hand up to the top their heads.

Moose—The child in the middle sticks her fingers up on the sides of her head as antlers. The kids to the sides put their outside hands to the side of their heads as ears.

Cow—The middle player interlocks his fingers and points his thumbs down, making an udder. The children on the sides make milking motions with middle person's thumbs.

Other ideas (have the kids decide how the character should look).

Dog
Cat
Eagle
Fish

■ Twizzle

This is a Simon Says... type of game with a literal *twist*. It is a good cognitive activity and teaches listening and following directions. It is also a lot of fun.

Play

Beginning Formation:

Large circle, with all the players facing the same direction.

Terminology:

GO — Walk in the direction that you are facing.

STOP — Stop moving and *freeze*!

TURN — Make a half turn (180°) and *freeze*!

JUMP — Jump and make a half turn (180°) and *freeze*!

TWIZZLE — Jump and make a full (360°) turn and *freeze*!

Give these instructions to the children. "The name of the game we are about to play is *Twizzle*. After we try some basic twizzling, we will attempt a couple rounds of *Competition Elimination Twizzle*—which is just plain old *Twizzle* with an arbitrary rule that eliminates you from the universe if you mess up."

Explain the terminology, then have your team practice each command as you loudly bark out a few, GO, STOPs and TURNs. The important thing to emphasize is that players must totally FREEZE after each command—with the exception, of GO. (Can't GO if you're frozen.)

After some practice time, play a game where no one is eliminated just to have some fun and practice. When you think everyone understands the rules and commands, announce that, "We are now going to play COMPETITION ELIMINATION TWIZZLE, but first we must all take the player's oath. So, raise your right foot and repeat after me."

"I (your name), do solemnly swear to do my best, to demonstrate the utmost honesty, sportsmanship, perseverance, and fair play while participating in this world renowned game of *COMPETITION ELIMINATION TWIZZLE!*

I promise that if it is discovered by the referees that I do not totally freeze in my tracks, and am therefore honestly eliminated from this game that I truly love, I will not moan, cry, whine, carry on, chastise or criticize.

"I promise to smile, laugh, and idiotically giggle upon being caught and to take my assigned and rightful new place in the center of the circle, thus positioning me to seek personal revenge and justification for having been so rudely snatched from my comfortable playing position.

"So it has been spoken. So it shall be done."

Arrange your students so that they are lined up in a circle and let the game begin.

When players are caught messing up, have them come to the middle of the circle and join you as a co-referees. If you hear grumblings or complaints, remind the transgressors about the oath just administered and accepted.

Continue playing until there are about 3-4 people left. Designate these lucky people as members of an elite group of Twizzle masters.

■ Wizards and Gelflings

This is a good warm-up, pre-practice activity that will definitely get your team loosened up.

In the universe (as defined by the boundaries of this game actually), there are two forces at work. Each force is represented by a unique species of beings. As is often the case when two species co-exist, there is tension and competition.

The first species is the Wizards. Wizards tend to be pretty serious because they are always thinking — creating spells, calculating formulas, analyzing experiments, chanting ancient rituals... They like their work a lot and don't like to be distracted.

On the other hand, Gelflings live to have FUN. They frolic, fantasize, sing, dance, merrily enjoying themselves without a care in the world. Well, almost not a care. They must watch out for Wizards.

Wizards have a fixated mindset about Gelflings. See a Gelfling, freeze it! Wizards constantly try to freeze Gelflings by touching them with their magic ball/wand/orb/hand.

As soon as a Gelfling is frozen, it immediately reacts to the suspension of its ability to frolic by emitting the Universal Gelfling Distress Call: a very high pitched wail (think of Tiny Tim doing "Tiptoe through the tulips..."), "Help Me, Help Me, Help Me ..."

A physical motion emphasizes this distress call. Use a fist with the thumb extended up, raising and lowering it into the palm of your other hand — the universally recognized Gelfling symbol for "help." This call repeats itself over and over until at least two unfrozen Gelflings surround their frozen partner, join hands and hug that person calling out, "Go free, little Gelfling, Go free." At this joyful juncture, the frozen Gelfling is free to frolic once again.

Wizards hate to see all their cryogenic work undone, so they get particularly upset as Gelflings become unfrozen. Wizards exhibit extra amounts of serious freezing energy when Gelflings congregate around a frozen partner.

The challenge in this activity is to find the proper balance between seriousness and fun. Too many Wizards, the game ends quickly and the Gelflings feel overwhelmed. Too few Wizards, the Gelflings get bored and the Wizards need CPR. Experiment with your team, but 2-3 Wizards for about 15-20 Gelflings seems to be an appropriate starting point.

One last suggestion; allow the Wizards to change their identity. Any time they get tired of chasing Gelflings, they can tag a Gelfling and then give them the Wizard's magic ball. The Gelfling is immediately transformed into a Wizard, the Wizard into a Gelfling. This technique has been proven to prevent major stress breakdowns in Wizards.

Appendix III

![square decoration]

A Brief History of Organized Youth Sports in America

Long before organized sports became popular in the United States, the idea that sports can build character was accepted in the British public schools (which were actually private secondary schools) during the mid-nineteenth century as a popular vehicle for promoting important social values. Students/athletes in these early games played an active role in organizing and governing their own games (a component often missing in adult-run youth sports programs in the United States). But equally important, the social norm of the time supported values such as camaraderie, fair play, and winning or losing gracefully. As sports were seen as a medium for promoting these qualities, there was a clear and logical connection between cultural philosophy and game practice.

When the idea of organized sports for school children was transported to the United States at the turn of the century, educators and parents believed that sport participation would promote pro-social values. Luther Gulick founded the Public Schools Athletic League (PSAL) on the basis of this idea, and in 1903 organized sports were brought into the school system. Initially organized sports programs centered on young boys, but in 1905 girls too began to participate in a limited program of exercise and activity in conjunction with PSAL.

Sports soon became an integral part of the school curriculum, and children's participation increased with little regard to whether the benefits of competitive sports outweighed their potential harm. But this question grew and the debate evolved into the more critical view that characterized the 1970s. One response was the introduction of New Games, which emphasized cooperation and participation while downplaying competition and selectivity. Cooperative sports offered an alternative "sports" experience for many children and adults. By the middle of the decade, educators and sports scientists had joined together in a more "specific" examination of what was taking place on American playing fields. The Youth Sports Task Force, of the National Association for Sport and Physical Education, developed its "Bill of Rights for Young Athletes" in 1976 to provide volunteers, whose numbers had grown by this time to 2.5 million, with guidelines for organizing and coaching young children while encouraging overall development.

The amount of information available about youth sports has increased considerably, but disseminating the results of research and coaching clinics has proved a problem for several reasons. First, understanding youth sports as an educational process is still a relatively new phenomenon, and many coaches are simply not up-to-date; the coaching community is, by and large, conservative. Many coaches are skeptical about new ideas, especially those coming from the research community. Secondly, while most coaches are willing to attend workshops, few are interested in attending the lengthy courses that lead to accreditation. A third problem arises in connecting theory to practice with models that actually work for coaches. Many researchers conduct theoretical studies of the sport environment, and they often have little application to performance on the field. Other studies discuss the issues of sport participation but lack the empirical validation of traditional research methods. Finally, current research and clinics are frequently geared to the volunteer coach and offer little to the professional, or they focus on techniques for improving athletes' performance rather than on understanding children. Halbert argues that "coaches of children need to know more about children. For example, how do children grow and develop? What motivates them? What are the best communication patterns to use…?"

—From *Learning for Life:*
Moral Education, Theory, and Practice

edited by Andrew Garrod

The PLUS Institute

---◼---

The Positive Learning Using Sports Institute is a non-profit organization which promotes sports as an educational medium for encouraging both athletic development and personal growth in school age children. Specifically the Institute serves four functions:

- To research how sports can encourage personal learning;

- To develop curricula for sports and academic programs;

- To provide programs for communities, schools, and parents;

- To serve as an educational resource center for schools, coaches, and parents.

At the PLUS Institute we believe sports can help children develop more than just athletic skills. Through sports, children can learn a great deal about themselves and others. Children can learn to share, to negotiate, to manage conflict, and understand human differences.

Through research at Harvard University, youth sports camps, and the classroom environment, the PLUS Institute develops educational curricula to teach positive values and interpersonal skills through sports. Our emphasis is on the young athlete as a learner. We make use of the best available psychological and educational research. The curricula can be applied in youth sports and recreational programs, schools, and the home.

For further information or to learn more about PLUS programs, contact:

The PLUS Institute
PO Box 219
New Hampton, NH 03256
603/744-5401 FAX: 603/744-3769

Project Adventure

Project Adventure, Inc. is a national, non-profit corporation dedicated to helping schools, businesses, and other groups implement Adventure programs.

Characterized by an atmosphere that is fun, supportive and challenging, Project Adventure programs use non-competitive games, group problem-solving Initiatives and ropes course events as the principal activities to help individuals reach their goals; to improve self-esteem, to develop strategies that enhance decision making, and to learn to respect differences within a group.

We conduct workshops around the country for teachers, counselors, youth workers and other professionals who work with people. Project Adventure has also been the leader in designing and constructing Challenge Ropes Courses since 1971.

To order additional copies of this book, there is an order form on the last page. Project Adventure publishes several other books that can also be useful to coaches of youth sports teams for teaching the principles of cooperation, trust, and teamwork. The activities contained in Appendix II originally appeared in *Youth Leadership in Action* and *QuickSilver*. These books also give information on some of the basics of Adventure Programming.

For further information about Project Adventure, call or write to:

Project Adventure, Inc.
PO Box 100
Hamilton, MA 01936
978/468-7981   FAX: 978/468-7605

■ *Youth Leadership In Action*

A Guide to Cooperative Games and Group Activities, Written by and for Youth Leaders

This is a compilation of Project Adventure's best games and activities written not only for youth leaders but written by youth leaders. In the book, the young authors tell their peers how they present the activities, what sorts of problems other youth leaders can expect and how to deal with them, and how to train and practice the activities before going out to lead them.

Youth Leadership In Action fills a long-neglected gap in the resources available to youth leaders, and will prove to be a valuable tool for any program that uses or wants to use youth leaders to their full potential.

Edited by Steve Fortier
$14.00

■ *QuickSilver*

Adventure Games, Initiative Problems, Trust Activities and a Guide to Effective Leadership

This latest offering from cooperative games master Karl Rohnke contains over 150 new games, problem solving initiatives, ice breakers, variations on old standards, trust, closures and more. There is also a section on leadership with co-author, Steve Butler, in which they impart many of the *secrets* that they use when leading and designing programs.

By Karl Rohnke and Steve Butler
$23.50

■ *Silver Bullets*

Since 1984, *Silver Bullets* has been the standard for the field of Adventure Education. Packed full of activities, cooperative games, stunts, and problem solving initiatives this book is an invaluable resource for anyone who wants to add some Adventure to their program.

By Karl Rohnke
$20.00

Order Form

Ship to:

Name _____

Address (no P.O. Box nos.) _____

_____

City _____ State _____ Zip _____

Phone (_____) _____ Ext _____

Due to the inability to trace Parcel Post shipments, it is our policy to ship U.S. orders via UPS.
We must have a UPS shipping address (no Post Office box numbers).

Book Rate will be used for orders sent to foreign countries and in cases of insufficient street addresses.

Payment: ❏ Check   ❏ Credit Card

❏ MasterCard   ❏ VisaCard   ❏ AmEx

Credit Card # _____ Exp. ___ / ___

Signature _____

(Signature required for all charge orders.)

☛ **TO ORDER PLEASE CALL: 800/795-9039**
FAX: 978/524-4600

or return this form to: **Project Adventure, Inc.**
P.O. Box 100
Hamilton, MA 01936

Qty.	Title	ISBN	Cost	Total
	Youth Leadership in Action	0107-3	14.00	
	QuickSilver	0032-8	23.50	
	Silver Bullets	5682-X	20.00	
	Sports PLUS	8713-3	16.00	

* **TAX-EXEMPT** orders must be accompanied by a copy of the purchaser's certificate of tax exemption.

How to Calculate Shipping Charges

■ **Add $4.00** for first book.
■ **Add .50¢** for each additional book up to 5 books.
■ **Over 5 books,** add 5% of total.

On books being shipped to AK, HI, Canada and foreign countries:
• 4.50 to Alaska & Hawaii
• 6.50 to Canada
• 7.00 on foreign orders
On orders of 5 or more books, call Project Adventure for exact shipping cost.

Subtotal _____

Please add sales tax:
GA add 6%
VT & MA add 5% _____

Tax Exempt No.* _____

Shipping (instructions at left) _____

TOTAL _____